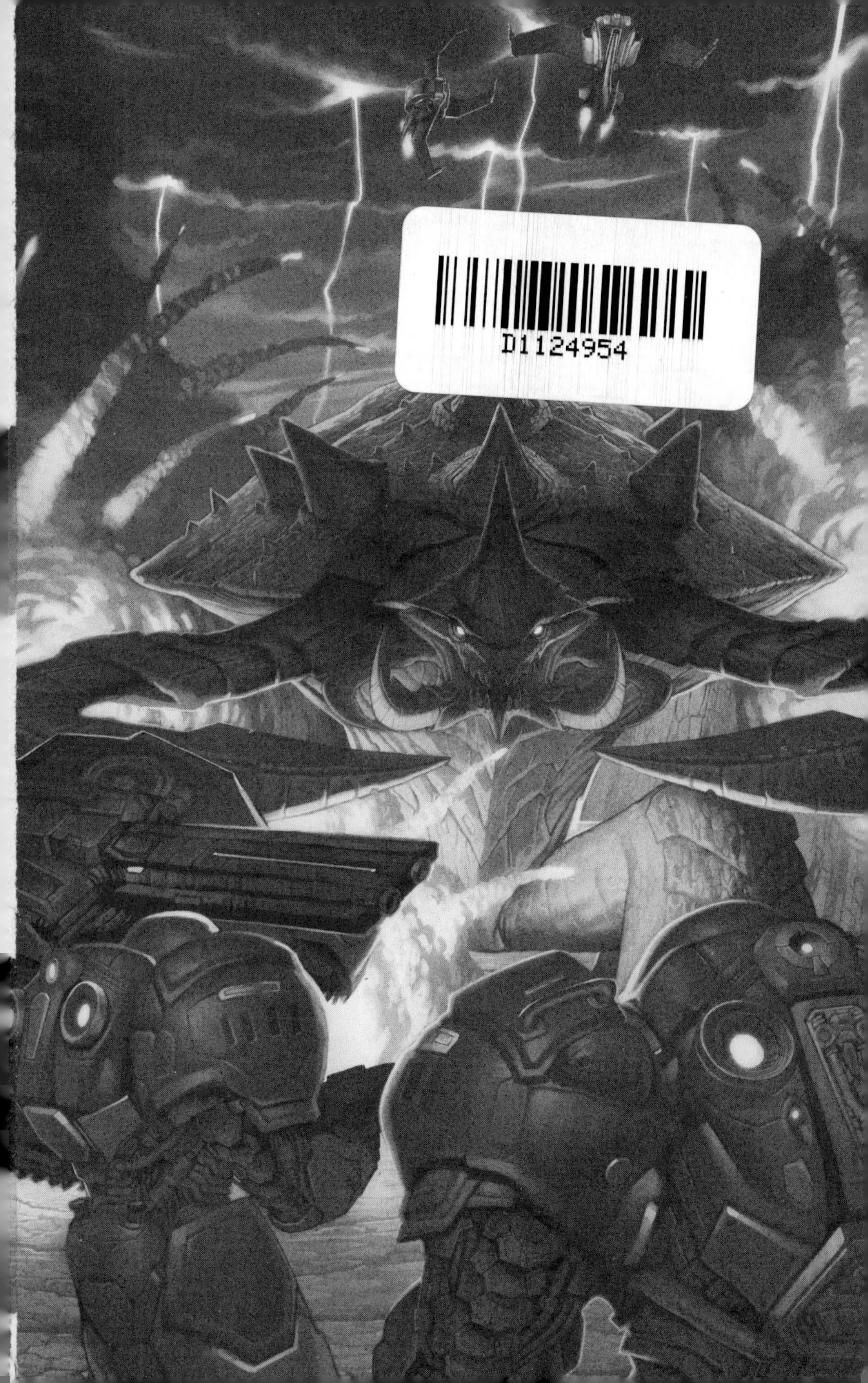

StarCraft: Frontline Vol. 2

Contributing Editor - Troy Lewter
Layout and Lettering - Michael Paolilli
Creative Consultant - Michael Paolilli
Graphic Designer - Louis Csontos
Cover Artist - UDON with Saejin Oh

Editor - Hope Donovan
Pre-Production Supervisor - Vicente Rivera, Jr.
Print-Production Specialist - Lucas Rivera
Managing Editor - Vy Nguyen
Senior Designer - Louis Csontos
Senior Designer - James Lee
Associate Publisher - Marco F. Pavia
President and C.O.O. - John Parker
C.E.O. and Chief Creative Officer - Stu Levy

BLIZZARD ENTERTAINMENT
Senior Vice President, Creative Development - Chris Metzen
Director, Creative Development - Jeff Donais
Lead Developer, Licensed Products - Shawn Carnes
Publishing Lead, Creative Development - Rob Tokar
Story Consultation and Development - Micky Neilson
Art Director - Glenn Rane
Director, Global Business Development and Licensing - Cory Jones
Associate Licensing Manager - Jason Bischoff
Additional Development - Samwise Didier, Evelyn Fredericksen, Ben Brode, Sean Wang, Bob Richardson

A TOKYOPOP Manga

TOKYOPOP and are trademarks or registered trademarks of TOKYOPOP Inc.

TOKYOPOP Inc.
5900 Wilshire Blvd. Suite 2000
Los Angeles, CA 90036

E-mail: info@TOKYOPOP.com
Come visit us online at www.TOKYOPOP.com

ISBN: 978-1-4278-0831-8

First TOKYOPOP printing: January 2009

10 9 8 7 6 5 4 3 2 1

Printed in the USA

STARCRAFT

FRONTLINE

VOLUME 2

HAMBURG // LONDON // LOS ANGELES // TOKYO

StarCraft

Frontline
Volume 2

StarCraft®

Frontline™
Volume 2

Heavy Armor – Part 2

Written by Simon Furman

Pencils and Inks by Jesse Elliott

Tones by Chi Wang, Marcus Jones and JC Padilla

Letterer: Michael Paolilli

PREVIOUSLY IN HEAVY ARMOR - PART 1

Viking pilot Wes Carter must protect a colony from his renegade mentor, Captain Jon Dyre—the man who taught him everything about heavy armor. During the military demonstration of a new Viking unit, Dyre went haywire, calling the colony infested and turning his black Viking on civilians! Carter successfully interrupted his mentor's rampage, but now must engage him in a deadly firefight...

NOW WHAT? DO I ENGAGE OR RUN?
I LOSE EVERY WHICH WAY IN A DIRECT HEAD-TO-HEAD. HIS VIKING HAS BETTER ARMOR, MORE OPTIONS, A FASTER RESPONSE TIME.
OH, AND IT'S IN THE HANDS OF THE MAN WHO WROTE THE BOOK ON GROUND COMBAT!

BUT IF I HIGHTAIL IT OUT OF HERE, HE MAY JUST DECIDE I'M NOT WORTH THE EFFORT AND HEAD BACK TO THE COLONY.

"KNOW YOUR TERRAIN." THAT WAS DYRE'S MANTRA. "KNOW YOUR TERRAIN."
TROUBLE IS, IT'S NO COINCIDENCE THE BRASS WANTED TO STAGE THE TEST ON URSA; IT'S WHERE DYRE FOUGHT HIS CAREER-MAKING CAMPAIGN, WIPING OUT A ZERG INFESTATION VIRTUALLY SINGLE-HANDEDLY.

HE ALREADY KNOWS THE LAY OF THE LAND. THE QUESTION IS...

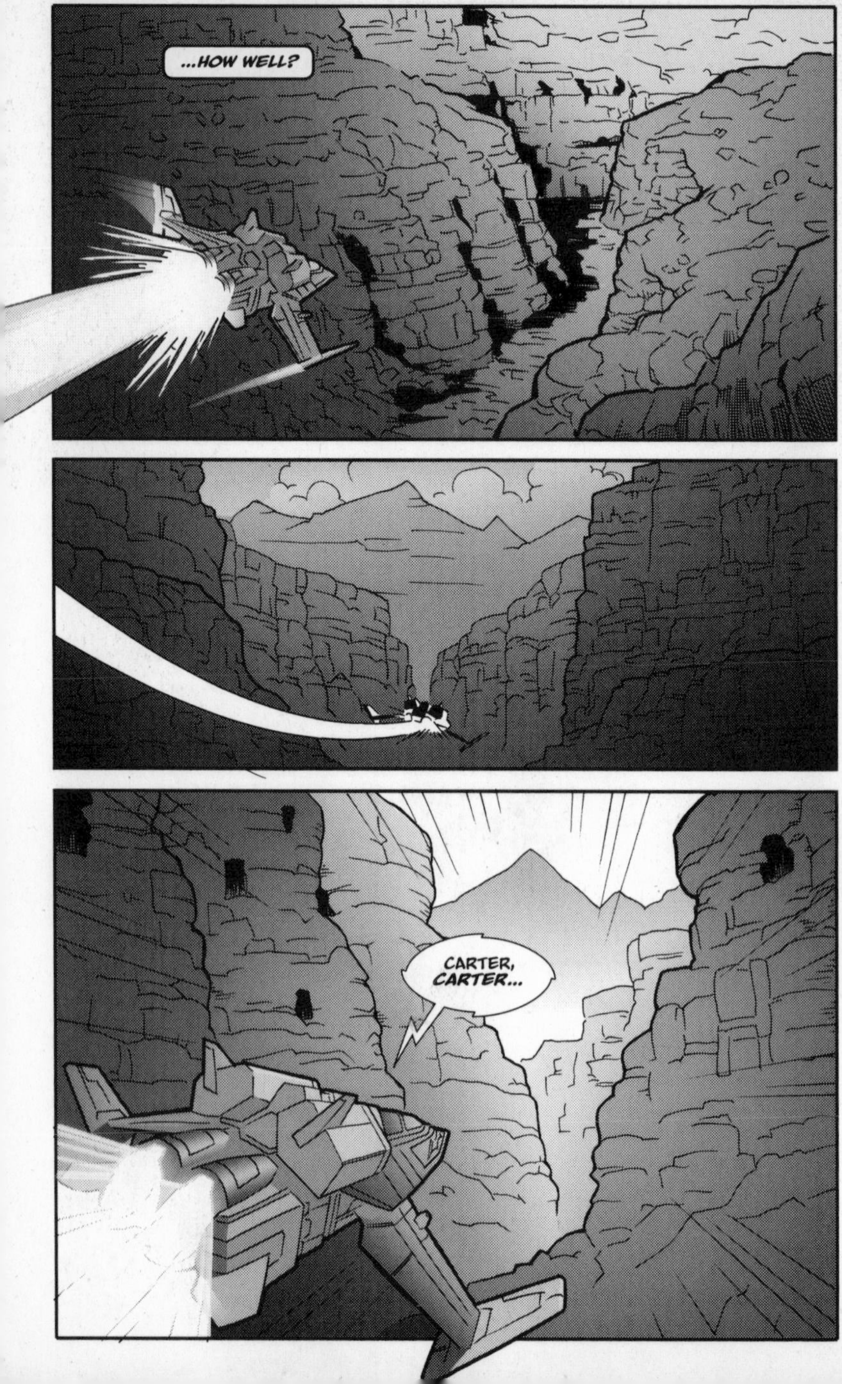

...HOW WELL?

CARTER,
CARTER...

...WHERE ARE YOU *GOING?*
THAT'S THE LAST PLACE YOU WANT TO BE.
HM. NO. YOU'RE *UP* TO SOMETHING. 
TACTICAL ADVANTAGE OF THE LOW GROUND IS ZERO.
WHICH MEANS THERE'S SOMETHING DOWN THERE YOU CAN USE.
BUT *WHAT?!*
THIS WHOLE AREA IS ONE BIG DUST BOWL. 
NO SURFACE VEGETATION, NO NATURAL COVER, NOTHING. NOWHERE TO HIDE, BUT...
...YOU *COULD* MAKE A LOW LEVEL RUN FOR THOSE MOUNTAINS, I SUPPOSE. MAYBE THAT'S IT.

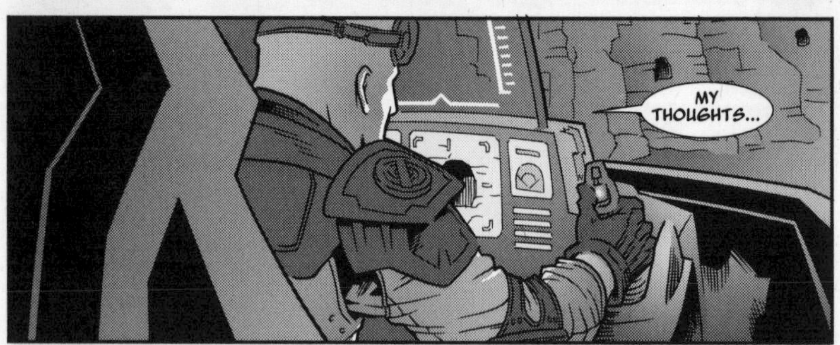

...EXACTLY!

VWUSH

THROOOSHAKT

DAAAAMN!
F-F-F-FULL MARKS, CARTER.
MANEUVERED ME RIGHT SMACK ON TOP OF A NATURAL GAS FIELD AND HIT IGNITION!
BUT I'VE ALREADY BEEN TO HELL, MORE THAN ONCE...

...AND LIVED TO TELL THE TALE.
TELL ME ABOUT THIS "CONTAMINATION," CAPTAIN.
WHERE'S YOUR INTEL COMING FROM?

MY 'INTEL' IS MY OWN TWO EYES.
INFESTED HUMANS, CARTER, NORMAL ONE MINUTE, SLAVERING ZERG HOSTS THE NEXT--SOME KIND OF EVOLUTION WE'VE NOT SEEN UNTIL HERE AND NOW!
YEAH?
DID YOU FILE A REPORT?

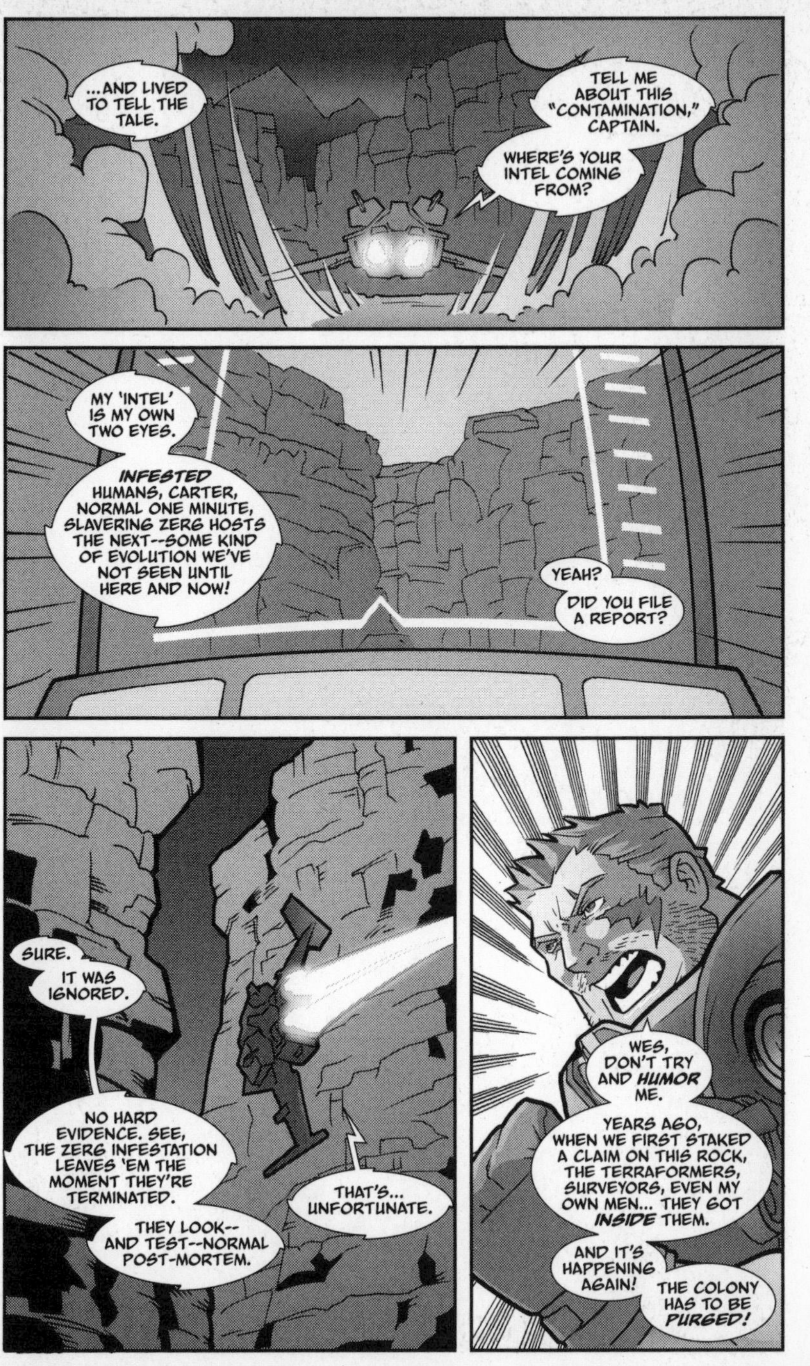

SURE.
IT WAS IGNORED.
NO HARD EVIDENCE. SEE, THE ZERG INFESTATION LEAVES 'EM THE MOMENT THEY'RE TERMINATED.
THEY LOOK--AND TEST--NORMAL POST-MORTEM.
THAT'S... UNFORTUNATE.
WES, DON'T TRY AND *HUMOR* ME.
YEARS AGO, WHEN WE FIRST STAKED A CLAIM ON THIS ROCK, THE TERRAFORMERS, SURVEYORS, EVEN MY OWN MEN... THEY GOT *INSIDE* THEM.
AND IT'S HAPPENING AGAIN!
THE COLONY HAS TO BE *PURGED!*

AND YOU...
ARE JUST A
DISTRACTION.
SWOOSH

SWIPP

VARAKK

I RIDE MY LUCK. BUT BITTER EXPERIENCE TEACHES EVERY SOLDIER, NO MATTER HOW TRENCH-SAVVY THEY MAY BE, LUCK RUNS OUT EVENTUALLY. DYRE'S ***RELENTLESS.***
IT'S ALL OR NOTHING NOW, ONE LAST THROW OF THE DICE. EVERYTHING RIDING ON DYRE...
...FORGETTING HIS ***OWN*** FIRST RULE!
I'M THROUGH RUNNING, CAPTAIN!
LET'S ***FINISH*** THIS...

...THE HEAVY ARMOR WAY.
SWLUT

SWOOP

VRRUM

VRRT
LET'S.

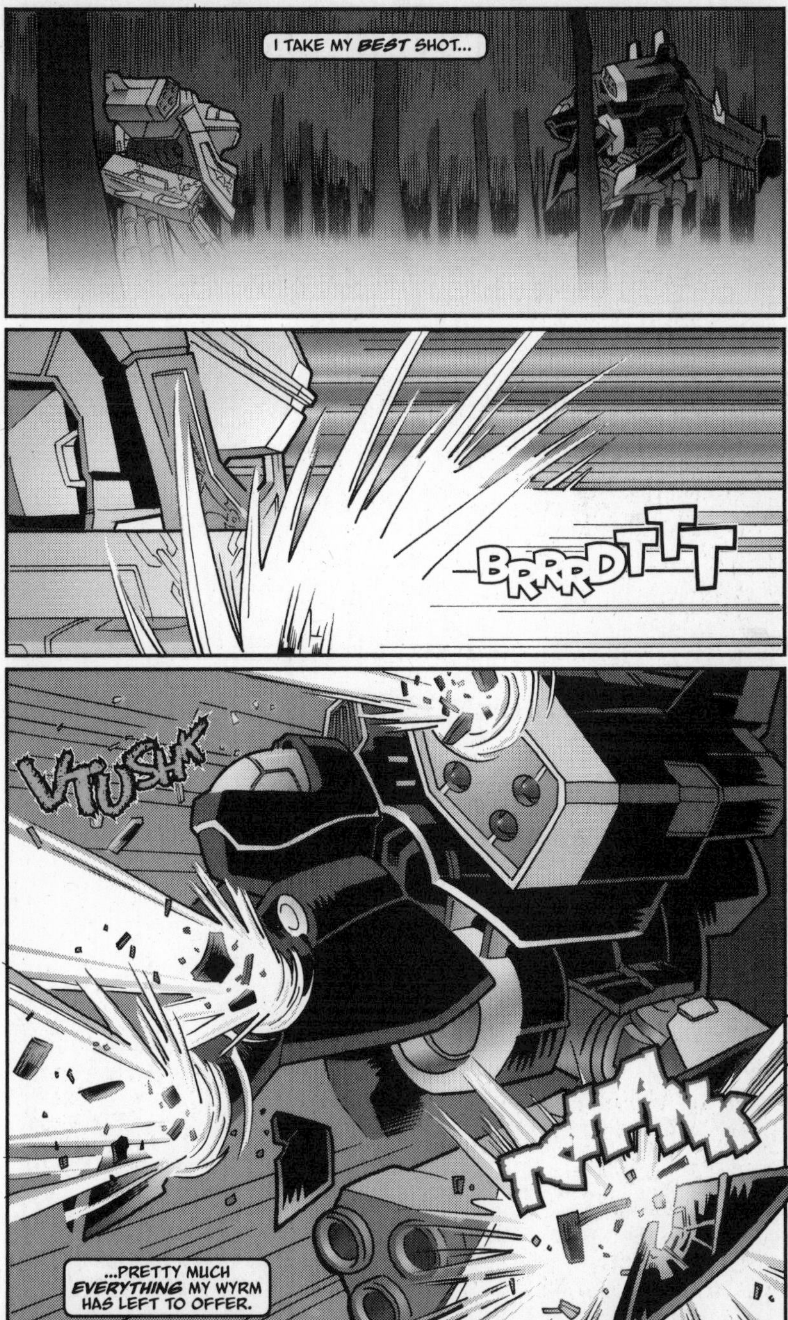

VTUSHK

TCHANK

...PRETTY MUCH ***EVERYTHING*** MY WYRM HAS LEFT TO OFFER.

IT'S NOWHERE NEAR ENOUGH.
FOR WHAT IT'S WORTH, CARTER...
...I'M SORRY IT HAS TO END THIS WAY.
ANY LAST WORDS?

STOMM!
BAKOW

ACTUALLY... YES.

KNOW YOUR TERRAIN.

EH?

SQUELCH

WHAT IS THIS?
CARTER?
CARTER!

IT'S CALLED TEMPA.
SEEMS SOLID ENOUGH, BUT IT'S NOT. IT'S LIKE QUICKSAND AND WET CONCRETE ALL ROLLED INTO ONE.
ONCE YOU'RE IN...
...THERE'S NO GETTING OUT.
KNOW WHAT I THINK, CARTER?
WHAT'S THAT, CAPTAIN?
I TAUGHT YOU WELL.
SIR, LISTEN TO ME.
I SWEAR I'LL LOOK INTO THIS NEW INFESTATION SCENARIO... I'LL LEAVE NO STONE UNTURNED.
BUT YOU HAVE TO POWER DOWN NOW AND SURRENDER YOUR ARMOR.
NO. I DON'T THINK SO.

SIR, YOU'RE *OUT* OF OPTIONS. PLEASE, WE CAN GET YOU HELP.
JUST NOW, YOU COULD HAVE TARGETED MY WYRM'S COCKPIT, BUT YOU DIDN'T.
IT'S NOT TOO LATE.

I...SHOULD *NEVER* HAVE COME BACK HERE, WES. THE THINGS I SAW, THE THINGS I HAD TO DO...

DO YOU KNOW *WHY* THEY SAY I WON THE BATTLE FOR URSA SINGLE-HANDED?

NO. WHY?

BECAUSE I *MASSACRED* EVERY SINGLE MAN AND WOMAN IN MY UNIT!

OH, IT WAS A BONA FIDE MERCY KILLING.
BUT THAT NEVER GOES AWAY. *NEVER.*
AND WES...

DRDIT-DRDIT-
DREEE-
...I DO STILL HAVE ONE *OTHER* OPTION!
EEEEEE-
NO!
PLEASE, NO! SIR, *ABORT* THE SEQUENCE!
ABORT--
CH-EEE-ZOW

THE CHIEF WANTS TO *BURY* THIS AND I DON'T BLAME HIM. I CERTAINLY HAVE NO WISH TO DRAG DYRE'S REPUTATION THROUGH THE MUD.
THE CORRUPTION IN HIM WAS NO LESS REAL, NO LESS PERNICIOUS, THAN AN ACTUAL ZERG INFESTATION.
INSTEAD OF FOLDING, HE SUBMERGED THE SHEER, UNRELENTING HORROR OF THAT DAY, LOCKED IT AWAY BEHIND HIS *OWN* HEAVY ARMOR.

DYRE FOUGHT HIS DEMONS AS LONG AND HARD AS HE COULD, AND THAT, ABOVE ALL ELSE...

...MAKES HIS ***MEMORY*** WORTH PRESERVING.

02
02
02
02

StarCraft

Frontline

Volume 2

Creep

Written by Simon Furman

Pencils by Tomás Aira
Inks by Tomás Aira and German Erramouspe
Tones by Tomás Aira, Wally Gomez and Ariel Lacci

Letterer: Michael Paolilli

Koprulu Sector
Protoss Advance/Experimental (P.A.X.) Facility

Protoss Zealots
Golarath
Ruom
Akam
I AM AKAM.
YOU ARE *FORTHUM.*
I AM.
ARE YOU PREPARED?

Protoss PAX Scientists
Jhas
WE ARE.
Harrum
Wa'Rak
Gruu
Forthum
THEN LET US NOT *DELAY.*

WE HAVE TAKEN EVERY PRECAUTION, AS OUR LEADERS SPECIFIED.
I WOULD EXPECT NO LESS.

...YOU AND YOUR ZEALOT BROTHERS WILL *REMAIN?*
IT WAS DEEMED PRUDENT, IN THE CIRCUMSTANCES.

YOU DISAPPROVE?

NOT IN THE LEAST. IT IS JUST--

YOU USUALLY DO YOUR WORK HERE IN *ISOLATION*. I UNDERSTAND. BUT, YOU SEE...

...THESE ARE MOST ASSUREDLY NOT USUAL CIRCUMSTANCES. NOT WHEN THE IMPENDING OBJECT OF YOUR ANALYTICAL MINISTRATIONS...

...IS THE CREEP.
THIS SAMPLE WAS PROCURED AT NO LITTLE COST. MANY WORTHY ZEALOTS DIED TO BRING IT THIS FAR. WE ARE HERE TO ENSURE NOTHING GOES...AWRY.

THE CREEP.
IN THE NEAR PROXIMITY OF IT, I STRUGGLE TO MAINTAIN MY CAREFULLY CONSTRUCTED RAMPARTS OF INTELLECTUAL DISPASSION.
BUT *CRACKS* START TO APPEAR.

HERE AT PAX, OUR THEOREMS AND STRATEGEMS CONFOUND ANY CONVENTIONAL SYSTEM OF CATEGORIZATION.
NOT SIMPLY PUSHING, BUT EXPLODING THE BOUNDARIES OF SCIENTIFIC EXPLORATION.
WE GO WHERE OTHERS FEAR TO TREAD, BEYOND THEORETICAL, BEYOND ETHICAL--
ARCHITECTS OF THE IMPOSSIBLE.
ZZAP
OUR DEMONSTRABLE LACK OF CONVENTION OR CONSCIENCE, THOUGH, MAKES US OUTCASTS, PARIAHS. OUR PEERS SHUN US, WHILE OUR LEADERS TURN A BLIND EYE.
BECAUSE WE HAVE OUR USES.

THESE EVOLVED CRYSTALS ACT AS A FAST COOLING MECHANISM. THE SAMPLE IS TO BE MAINTAINED AT A TEMPERATURE YOUR WARRIORS MAY FIND... UNCOMFORTABLE!
I SEE.
BUT UNDERSTAND... RUOM AND GOLARATH ARE TO HAVE CONTINUAL AND READY ACCESS TO THE SAMPLE.
I DO NOT--
OUR SUPERIORS WISH THE EXPERIMENT INDEPENDENTLY MONITORED AT ALL STAGES!
SO THAT PAST MISTAKES ARE NOT REPEATED.
CASE IN POINT, THE CREEP.
IT DEFINES THE ZERG'S POTENTIAL FOR AGGRESSIVE COLONIZATION...AND YET WE HAVE BARELY SCRATCHED THE SURFACE.
IT IS A LIVING CARPET OF BIO-MATTER, PROVIDING THE ZERG WITH BOTH INFRASTRUCTURE AND NOURISHMENT. UNCHECKED, IT SPREADS LIKE WILDFIRE. ALL THIS WE KNOW.

...IS GENOCIDE.

GLOORK

END THE ZERG THREAT FOREVER.

HAVING COMPLETED AN EXHAUSTIVE SERIES OF MENTAL MINING EXPEDITIONS, PAVING THE WAY FOR THE INTRODUCTION OF THE *VIRUS CULTURE* ITSELF...
...I RETURN TO MY CELL FOR PERSONAL CONTEMPLATION.
BUT INSTEAD OF A BRIGHT, REVIVIFYING VOID...
...I FIND A LONG-INTERRED *MEMORY.*
A MEMORY OF ***BROTHER NUBAS*** AND HIS ILL-FATED GENE-KEY. THE PROPOSITION WAS SOUND--THE UNLOCKING/ ACCELERATION OF PROTOSS GENETIC POTENTIAL--BUT HE CHOSE TO SHORTCUT HIS OWN ASSERTION...
...BY EXPERIMENTING ON *HIMSELF.*

WE LATER DISCOVERED THAT A FUNDAMENTAL HELIX STRAND WAS *MISSING* A KEY SEQUENCE.
SLOOOOSHHH
COLD COMFORT FOR BROTHER NUBAS.
A LESSON FOR THE REST OF US.
WHAT NATURE OR KHAS HAS GIVEN US, WE ENHANCE, STREAMLINE, UPGRADE--MAKING OUR RACE BETTER, FASTER, *STRONGER*.
WE PROPOSE, WE TEST, WE INSTIGATE.

AND WHEN WE REACH LIMITS, SELF-IMPOSED OR OTHERWISE...

...WE GO *FURTHER.*
UNTIL...?

WHAT? HOW DOES ONE TOP THE COMPLETE AND UTTER ERADICATION OF AN ENTIRE SPECIES? ARE WE, COLLECTIVELY, JUST LIKE BROTHER NUBAS...
...AN *ACCIDENT* WAITING TO HAPPEN?

WOOSH
WOOSH
THEN, OUT OF NOWHERE...
...WE ARE PLUNGED INTO A NIGHTMARE.
WHAT HAPPENED HERE? AKAM!
RUOM AND GOLARATH WENT IN TO EXTRACT TISSUE FROM THE SAMPLE. I REMAINED OUTSIDE. AND THEN...
...I DO NOT KNOW. THE CREEP JUST ERUPTED!
IT WAS EVERYWHERE! ALL OVER RUOM AND GOLARATH...THEN GOLARATH JUST...
GLUP
OOZE
...STARTED DISFIGURING HIMSELF! BEFORE I COULD GET TO HIM, HE HAD FALLEN ON HIS OWN PSI-BLADES!

AND RUOM...
...IS JUST *UNREADABLE.*
HIS MIND IS A TORRENT OF CONTRADICTORY AND NONSENSICAL IMAGERY.
BUT *UNDERNEATH* THEM, SOMETHING...
YES. YES.
HIS FREEFALL THOUGHTS ARE OVERWHELMING.
FEAR. DREAD. A PRESENCE...
ENOUGH!
HOW DID THIS HAPPEN? *HOW?!*
AKAM, I UNDERSTAND YOUR ANGER, BUT NO ONE IS TO *BLAME* HERE. ALL WE CAN DO...
...IS SEE TO RUOM.
YES. YES.
HE WILL NEED TO BE *QUARANTINED.* IN CASE THERE ARE FURTHER ILL-EFFECTS.

STRANGE.

THROUGH THE *PSIONIC LINK* WE ALL SHARE, GOLARATH AND RUOM'S LAST THOUGHTS SHOULD BE OURS...

...AND THEY ARE *NOT*.

IT IS *HIM*.

HE HAS COME BACK.

BROTHER NUBAS.

BROTHER JHAS IS RIGHT. IN FACT...I SENSE A GENERAL FOG WHERE USUALLY THERE IS FINE CRYSTAL CLARITY. AS IF...

BROTHER HARRUM...
...WHAT DO YOU MEAN, "HE IS BACK"?
I MEAN, HE IS BACK. TO SEE US ALL SUFFER...
...FOR WHAT WE DID TO HIM.
WHAT DID HE MEAN?
NO ONE FORCED NUBAS TO PUMP HIMSELF FULL OF EXPERIMENTAL DRUGS AND SEAL HIMSELF IN A NUTRIENT TANK!
AH! I DO NOT HAVE TIME FOR THIS...!
RUOM'S WELFARE IS MY SOLE CONCERN!
HARRUM'S OUTBURST... CURIOUS THAT IT SHOULD COINCIDE WITH MY OWN ROGUE MEMORY!

ALONE LATER, I FEEL A STRANGE IMPERATIVE TO CLOSE MY MIND TO SENSORY INPUT, AS IF RESISTING A DEATHLY MALAISE HOVERING--PREDATORY--ON THE BORDERS OF CONSCIOUSNESS.
INSTEAD, I SEEK OUT LIFE, ALBEIT IN THE ARTIFICIALLY MAINTAINED CONFINES OF THE *VIVARIUM.*

AND I AM NOT THE ONLY ONE.
BROTHER GRUU!
BROTHER WA'RAK.

WE MUST PREPARE OURSELVES.

PREPARE FOR *WHAT,* WA'RAK?

FOR THE POSSIBILITY THAT WHILE BROTHER NUBAS' PHYSICAL FORM SURELY PERISHED...

...HIS MIND DID *NOT!*

YOU HAVE FELT IT TOO. HIS... PRESENCE.
HE HAS RETURNED TO *JUDGE* US.
I DO NOT UNDERSTAND. CLARIFY.

OUR SIN. OUR TRANSGRESSION.
THE WARPED, TWISTED THINGS WE BIRTHED AND ABANDONED ALONG THE PATH TO THE PROTOSS IDEAL.
PREPARE.

PREPARE!

MY FIRST INCLINATION IS TO DISMISS WA'RAK'S OUTBURST AS MERELY ANOTHER SYMPTOM OF WHATEVER CURRENTLY AILS PAX. *BUT...*

...WHAT IF NUBAS' GENE-KEY ELEVATED HIS CONSCIOUSNESS TO A STATE *BEYOND* THE PHYSICAL? AND "DEATH"...

...WAS JUST THE *BEGINNING?*

DASH
BROTHER JHAS? WHAT...?
DID YOU NOT SENSE IT? THE DISTURBANCE?

PAX Hub

CRACKLE

CAN IT BE *STOPPED?*

NO.

THE REACTION HAS ALREADY PROGRESSED BEYOND CRITICAL. SOMEONE KNEW *EXACTLY* WHAT TO BREAK.

ZZZT

ZZT

RRRUMMMBBLE

KHAS HELP US!

KRSZZZT
KRRAKL

FLASH
KA-THOOOM

KRAK
KRRAKL
BZZZPT

BA-THWOOOM
SHUUUKKK

CRUSHING, INWARD, VORTEX--

THE GATE. **GONE.**

CLINK CLINK

IS EVERYONE...?

WE WILL HEAL.

YOU THINK... THIS WAS **DELIBERATE?**

SABOTAGE?

I **KNOW** IT.

NO GATE.
NO PYLON.
NO WAY OUT!
WHERE ARE THE *OTHERS?* HARRUM? WA'RAK?
SOMETHING IS WRONG... WITHIN THE *KHALA!* IT IS AS IF WE ARE SHROUDED IN A FOG, AND WE ARE BLIND AND STUMBLING WITHIN.
I... CANNOT SENSE HARRUM *AT ALL!* AND WA'RAK... DESOLATION... PAIN... TERRIBLE, CRUSHING BURDEN, UNBEARABLE...
DASH
HIS QUARTERS-- *MAKE HASTE!*
WA'RAK. I SENSE...
...WE ARE ALREADY TOO LATE.

DEATH HOLDS NO MYSTERIES FOR THE PROTOSS. WE FEEL EACH TRANSFIGURATION IN PATTERNS OF THOUGHT THAT TRANSCEND DESCRIPTION.
WE ARE NEVER SURPRISED.
BUT, IN WAYS I CANNOT QUANTIFY, EVERYTHING IS DIFFERENT NOW.
IT IS LIKE GOLARATH...ALL OVER AGAIN! HE...

...DID THIS TO *HIMSELF!* MUTILATED HIS OWN *NERVE-APPENDAGES.*
WHY?
WHY?
HIS... GUILT... IS PALPABLE.
IT DRIPS FROM EVERY WOUND. *HE* DESTABILIZED THE *HUB.*

...AND SAT BACK AND LET HIS DNA COOK!
...IT IS NOT THE FIRST TIME!
...AND YET IT IS. AND...
EXCEPT... THAT IS NOT HOW IT HAPPENED...
HOW MUCH?
HOW MUCH BLOOD ON THESE HANDS?
ENOUGH!
YOU THREE REMAIN HERE. WHATEVER THE TRUTH OF THE MATTER, I INTEND TO UNCOVER IT.
SOMEONE WANTED US ISOLATED, VULNERABLE, AND I--

SLICE
SSHLIK

ZEALOT RUOM HAS SUCCUMBED. BUT...
INFESTED!
THAT IS IMPOSSIBLE! THE FORTITUDE OF THE KHALA IS SUCH THAT WE CANNOT BE INFESTED. UNLESS, SOMEHOW...
THUD
...THE CREEP ITSELF HAS EVOLVED!
IT...IS AN ABOMINATION!
IT HAS TO BE DESTROYED! IF THE CREEP IS "WITHIN," ALL PROTOSS ARE IMPERILLED!
JHAS, NO! DON'T--
AH!!
SHUNK
SPLIK

EIAAA!!
JHAS!
SPLORCH
HE IS BEYOND OUR HELP. WE...
...DESERVE TO DIE. THOSE FACES, THOSE PITIFUL PLEADING FACES! I-I AM...SORRY. SO, SO SORRY!
MOVE.
"IT"? I DO NOT--
CAN YOU NOT SEE? IT HAS DONE THIS TO US. IT IS INSIDE OUR HEADS!
GLOORP

LUNGE
FORTHUM! WATCH OUT!
SLASH
HHOK!
THWAK
NEVER MAKE IT... MAY AS WELL...
...ACCEPT OUR FATE!
NO! PERHAPS...
IF I CAN JUST...
WHAT?
WHAT DID YOU DO?
FLIKKER

T-TELEPORTATION MECHANISM...IN RUOM'S ARMOR!
I *ACTIVATED* IT WITH A MENTAL PUSH.
H-HOW FAR?
NOT FAR ENOUGH.
STOMP STOMP
STOMP
INFESTED. IT ALL MAKES A KIND OF SKEWED SENSE. *WE* DID THIS.
THE CREEP.
SENTIENT. EVOLVED. MUTATED INTO A *PSIONIC PREDATOR.*
THAT IS WHY GOLARATH AND WA'RAK MUTILATED THEMSELVES--TO PROTECT US!
THE CREEP-INDUCED MADNESS IS *SPREADING,* VIA OUR NERVE APPENDAGES. AND IT IS GROWING EVER STRONGER!

EVEN ARMED WITH THIS KNOWLEDGE...
I CANNOT. I CANNOT.
STUMBLE
...THE SEARING HORROR IS PALPABLE.
I SEE MYSELF...
...AND A NAMELESS MASS, BUTCHERED IN THE NAME OF SCIENCE. SO MANY BODIES, AND TRY AS I MIGHT...
FOOM
...I CANNOT GET RID OF THEM ALL.

FALSE MEMORIES, PERHAPS. BUT SO DEEPLY ROOTED...
...THEY MAY AS WELL BE *REAL*.
THE NEARER WE GET TO THE POSTULATORIUM...
NO! *NO!*
WHAT ARE YOU DOING? THEY ARE RIGHT *THERE*, WAITING FOR US! *STOP!*
...THE WORSE IT BECOMES.
I AM SORRY. I NEVER MEANT...
NEVER THOUGHT...
SCRAMBLE
POOR FORTHUM.
I KNOW *EXACTLY* HOW HE FEELS.

DASH
RUOM!
SHUNK
JUST *ME* NOW. ME...

...AND *THE CREEP.*

HOW DID THIS *HAPPEN?* HOW DID THE CREEP METAMORPHOSE INTO THIS PSIONIC PREDATOR?

PERHAPS IT WAS THE VIRAL AGENT ITSELF...OR MAYBE ONCE IT WAS *INSIDE* RUOM, IT UPGRADED. CHANCES ARE...

...WE'LL *NEVER* KNOW!

ONE THING FOR SURE, THERE IS NOT MUCH TIME.

GLOOP

GLUP

GLOOP

FINDING IT HARDER AND HARDER JUST TO *THINK...* EITHER MY OWN CANCEROUS PSYCHE WILL CLAIM ME...OR THE *INFESTED* RUOM!

I HAVE NO ILLUSIONS.
NO ONE GETS OUT ALIVE.

I CAN FEEL IT IN MY HEAD, EXPOSING AND EXPLOITING EVERY WEAKNESS, SEEDING GUILTY SECRETS, PUSHING ME EVER CLOSER TO THE ABYSS.
BLOORK
BUT MY SHAME AND THE CREEP ARE ONE AND THE SAME.
I OPENED THE THEORETICAL DOOR TO GENOCIDE. MY FORWARD STRATEGEM LED TO THE SAMPLE BEING BROUGHT TO PAX. IT WAS ME...
...ALL ME!
TWITCH

...AS A WAY *OUT.*

WOBBLE

WOBBLE

BLGOOK

EVEN NOW IT SEEMS, MY EFFORTS TO DO THE RIGHT THING...

...ARE DESTINED TO FAIL.
ZOOOMM
THIS PLACE IS, AND ALWAYS WAS...
...A DEAD END!
ZZIT
ADUN GRANT ME THE COURAGE TO SHATTER THE COOLING CRYSTALS AND FREEZE INTO OBLIVION THIS HANDIWORK!
BYEEEOW
KRAAKKL
KRAAKKL
KRRTCH

KRAAAK
PWOOOOOOM
KRRRTCH
KRAAKL
TINK
TINK
KRAAAK
KRRTCH

KRAAKL
KRRTCH
FWOOOOOOO
KRRTCH
KRAAKL
TINK
TINK
KRAAKL

Later...

YES, SIR. WE HAVE *REACHED* THE OBJECTIVE.

STATUS?
STAND BY...

WELL?
SIR, THE CREEP SAMPLE...

...APPEARS STILL *VIABLE.*

RIGHT. PREP FOR *IMMEDIATE* EXTRACTION...

END

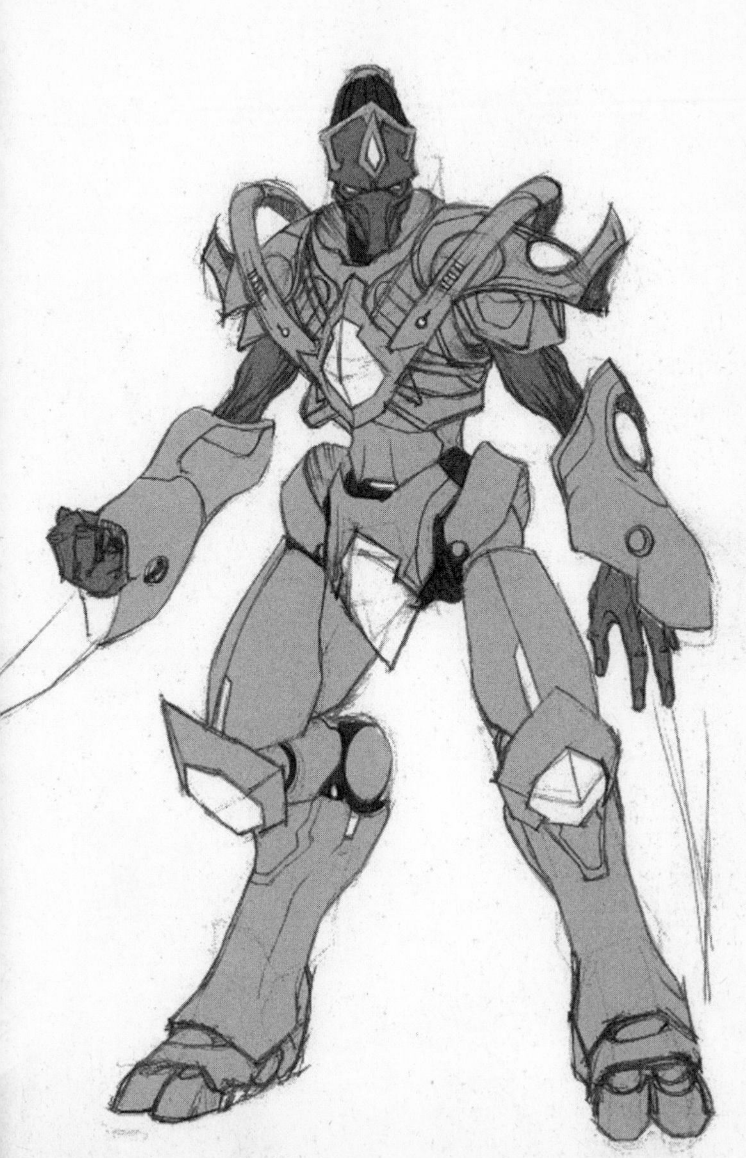

STARCRAFT

FRONTLINE

VOLUME 2

NEWSWORTHY

Written by Grace Randolph

Art by Nam Kim
Inks by Matt Dalton
Tones by Studioil
Studioil Staff: AJ Ford 3, Ben Harvey & Shiwah Wong

Letterer: Michael Paolilli

UNN
UNIVERSE NEWS NETWORK
WELCOME BACK!
IF YOU'RE JUST JOINING US, WE'RE TALKING TO UNIVERSAL NEWS NETWORK'S OWN STAR REPORTER KATE LOCKWELL, WHO...
NEWS

...IS ABOUT TO EMBARK ON AN EXCLUSIVE ASSIGNMENT!
THAT'S RIGHT, TOM.
RIGHT AFTER I LEAVE THIS VERY STUDIO, I'LL BE JOINING AN ACTUAL DOMINION MARINE CORPS BATTALION...
...AND DOCUMENTING ONE OF THEIR MISSIONS.

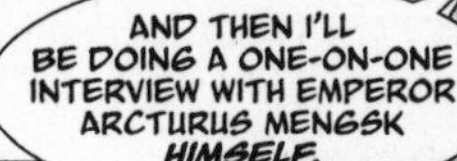
AND THEN I'LL BE DOING A ONE-ON-ONE INTERVIEW WITH EMPEROR ARCTURUS MENGSK HIMSELF.

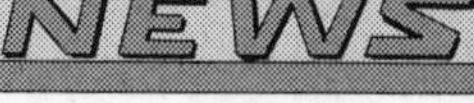
NEWS

AND YOU CAN SEE BOTH STORIES NEXT MONTH...
...AS WE AT UNN MARK THE ANNIVERSARY OF THE EMPEROR'S INAUGURATION!

NICE.
VERY NICE.
YOU FOLKS AT UNN HAVE BEEN PLAYING THAT ALL WEEK.
THIS IS A BIG STORY FOR US.
THE DOMINION HASN'T ALLOWED AN EMBEDDED REPORTER SINCE--
MICHAEL LIBERTY.
AND HE LEFT QUITE A SCAR.
I'M NOT INTO TABLOID JOURNALISM, MAJOR HAWKINS.
I'M HERE TO DELIVER THE NEWS.
I KNOW YOU ARE, LOCKWELL.

I KNOW YOU ARE, BECAUSE YOUR EDITOR-IN-CHIEF, MR. HANDY ANDERSON, VOUCHED FOR YOU.
WE'VE BEEN WARY OF UNN AFTER THAT MESS WITH LIBERTY, BUT ANDERSON *PROMISED* US THAT WOULDN'T HAPPEN AGAIN.
NO MORE FANATICAL NUT JOBS WHO STAB US IN THE BACK THEN TAKE A FLYING LEAP OFF THE GRID.
PROBLEM WAS, MICHAEL LIBERTY ONLY SAW FIT TO TELL THINGS THE WAY *HE* SAW 'EM.
WE'RE LOOKING FOR SOMEONE TO TELL THINGS THE WAY THE *DOMINION MARINE CORPS* SEES 'EM.
AND YOU'VE ALWAYS DONE GOOD BY THE DOMINION, WHICH WE MARINES SURE DO APPRECIATE.
WHEN I'M DONE, ALL OF THE DOMINION'S PEOPLE WILL APPRECIATE THE MARINES.
THERE'S A LOT AT STAKE HERE, LOCKWELL. FOR BOTH OF US.
AN EXCLUSIVE LIKE THIS...IT COULD MAKE YOUR CAREER.
I'M WELL AWARE OF THAT, MAJOR.

DO YOU FIND YOUR QUARTERS SATISFACTORY, MS. LOCKWELL?

YES, PRIVATE, I DO.

BEEP

IF IT'S NOT TOO FORWARD OF ME, MA'AM...

...I'D LIKE TO SAY "THANK YOU" FOR WHAT YOU'RE DOING TO HELP THE DOMINION MARINE CORPS.

WSHHHH!

NO "THANKS" NECESSARY.

THE MAJOR WANTED ME TO INFORM YOU WE'LL BE DEPARTING FROM THE STARPORT SHORTLY.

GOOD TO HEAR.

LET'S GET THIS PARTY STARTED--

MY THOUGHTS *EXACTLY.*

WHAT ARE *YOU* DOING HERE?!
UH, I'M YOUR *CAMERAMAN*.
NO YOU'RE *NOT!*
I FIRED YOUR ASS MONTHS AGO!

YOU'RE GETTING OFF THIS SHIP RIGHT NOW!!

THEN YOU'VE GOT NO STORY.

I'M SORRY TO REPORT YOUR REGULAR CAMERAMAN HAS COME DOWN WITH A COLD.

A VERY *EXPENSIVE* ONE, I MIGHT ADD.

WE'LL HAVE FUN! IT'LL BE *JUST* LIKE OLD TIMES!

YOU MIGHT HAVE "FIRED MY ASS," BUT THAT DOESN'T ERASE *FIVE YEARS* OF HISTORY.

I TAKE IT YOU'RE STILL INTO BULLSHIT CONSPIRACY THEORIES.

WELL, I DON'T KNOW ABOUT THE BULLSHIT PART, BUT YEAH.

DAMMIT, THERE ISN'T TIME TO GET ANOTHER CAMERAMAN...
LISTEN, THIS IS THE FIRST EMBEDDED ASSIGNMENT IN YEARS!
HOW COULD I PASS UP A CHANCE TO TAKE A PEEK BEHIND THE IRON CURTAIN?
THERE IS NO "IRON CURTAIN."
THAT'S YOUR OPINION.
CAREER GOALS ASIDE, THESE SOLDIERS ARE GOOD MEN WHO PUT THEIR LIVES ON THE LINE FOR UNGRATEFUL SCUM LIKE YOU.
I WON'T HAVE YOU MAKING A JOKE OUT OF THIS ASSIGNMENT.
KATE...I JUST WANT TO MAKE SURE THE JOKE ISN'T ON THEM.

WE'RE STANDING IN THE CONTROL ROOM OF A BRAND NEW *MINOTAUR*-CLASS BATTLECRUISER.
WHILE THE BROOD WAR TOOK A HEAVY TOLL ON US, YOU CAN SEE THAT THE DOMINION MARINE CORPS IS BACK, BETTER THAN EVER.

REC●
HERE IS WHERE OUR BRAVE ENLISTED MARINES GET THEIR REST.
HOW'S THAT MATTRESS, PRIVATE?
0
REC●
SOFT AS A BABY'S BEHIND, SIR.
0
HMPH
AND THIS IS WHERE OUR YOUNG MEN CAN GET A GOOD HOT MEAL.
WHY, FRIENDSHIPS THAT LAST A LIFETIME ARE FORGED AT THESE VERY TABLES.
BUT A MARINE'S WORK IS NOT ALL FUN AND GAMES--HE HAS A DUTY AS WELL...

...AND THAT DUTY IS TO EVERY PLANET IN THE TERRAN DOMINION, NO MATTER HOW SMALL.
IF YOU'RE WITH THE TERRAN DOMINION, THEN YOU'RE FAMILY.
AND FAMILY PROTECTS FAMILY.
BE IT BRINGING IMPORTANT SUPPLIES...
...OR CHECKING THE SURROUNDING AREA FOR SIGNS OF THE ENEMY, SUCH AS THE ZERG!

WHAT MADE YOU JOIN THE DOMINION MARINES, SON?
I WANT TO SAVE PEOPLE, SIR.
THAT WAS A GREAT LINE AT THE END, MAKE SURE YOU USE THAT.
BUT YOU CAN LOSE THE "BABY'S BEHIND" REMARK FROM EARLIER.
WE DON'T NEED PEOPLE THINKING THIS IS A FLOATING COLONY OF PERVERTS.
HOW ARE WE DOING?
MEMORY'S ALMOST FULL.
I NEED TO SWITCH OUT.
WHAT, *NOW?*
WE'RE ALREADY PLANETSIDE, SIR, AND IT'S URGENT.
WELL THAT'S JUST *GREAT...*

LOOK, LOCKWELL, WE'RE GOING TO HAVE TO LEAVE YOU AND YOUR CAMERAMAN HERE FOR A FEW HOURS.
TACTICAL HAS ASSIGNED US TO A MISSION NEARBY.
REALLY? WE'D LOVE TO COVER IT!
NO CAN DO.
BUT IT SHOULDN'T TAKE TOO LONG AND WE'LL BE BACK TO PICK YOU UP SHORTLY.
BESIDES, DIDN'T YOU SAY YOU HAD FOOTAGE TO DOWNLOAD?
I'VE INSTRUCTED SOME OF MY MEN TO SET UP YOUR EQUIPMENT IN A TENT.
WOOSH

WHY COULDN'T WE GO WITH THEM AGAIN?
WHATEVER. THE USUAL.
"FOR OUR OWN PROTECTION."
"IT'S CLASSIFIED"...

YOUR TENT'S READY.

WHAT ARE YOU DOING?

BACKING UP THE FOOTAGE.
I THINK YOU MEAN COPYING.
HEY, I'M JUST DOING MY JOB.
CLICK
BESIDES, ON A STORY LIKE THIS, IT'S BETTER SAFE THAN SORRY.
WHAT'S THAT SUPPOSED TO MEAN?
COME ON, YOU KNOW. MARINES DON'T LIKE SOMETHING WE TAPE, THEY CAN CONFISCATE THE FOOTAGE.
THAT IS EXACTLY THE KIND OF ATTITUDE THAT COULD JEOPARDIZE THIS STORY.
KATE, DON'T KID YOURSELF.
THERE'S NO STORY TO JEOPARDIZE.

I'D LIKE TO GO BACK TO THE COLONY AND INTERVIEW THE COLONISTS.
AND I'D LIKE TO NOT BE BABYSITTING SOME CHICK REPORTER AND HER FLUNKIE.
WISHFUL THINKING ON BOTH OUR PARTS, BABE.
EXCUSE ME...?!
MISSION'S COMPLETED, BUT LOOKS LIKE WE'RE HEADING BACK TO 'PORT.
TRANSPORT SHIP'LL BE HERE IN A FEW MINUTES. LET'S PACK UP.

...THERE'S NOT ENOUGH ROOM.
BUT SIR, THE BRIG SIMPLY ISN'T BIG ENOUGH.
THIS IS NOT SOMETHING TO DISCUSS IN FRONT OF CIVILIANS.
HANDLE IT.
GOOD TO SEE YOU AGAIN, LOCKWELL!
ARE THERE PRISONERS ONBOARD?
...SORRY, LOCKWELL. STORY'S OVER.
BUT I WAS SUPPOSED TO INTERVIEW YOU!
ENJOY OUR HOSPITALITY ON THE FLIGHT BACK TO 'PORT.

THIS FOOD'S ACTUALLY PRETTY GOOD...
DAMMIT! YOU'RE RIGHT... WE HAVE *NO STORY!*
NO, BUT I'M PRETTY SURE ONE'S SITTING DOWN THERE IN THE *BRIG*.
QUESTION IS, WHAT ARE YOU GOING TO DO ABOUT IT?
GET MY INTERVIEW...!
ARE YOU SURE IT'S OKAY FOR YOU TO INTERVIEW ME?
OF COURSE! BESIDES, I BET YOUR FAMILY WILL BE PRETTY EXCITED TO SEE YOU ON TV!
UH, YEAH...
OKAY, WE'RE READY TO ROLL.

SURE I'M GLAD I JOINED THE DOMINION MARINE CORPS.
IT'S NICE TO BE A PART OF SOMETHING BIGGER THAN MYSELF, Y'KNOW?
AND THAT'S BECAUSE YOU'RE FIGHTING SOMETHING BIGGER THAN YOURSELF, RIGHT?
WHO'S LOCKED UP DOWN IN THE BRIG?
WHAT? UH, I DON'T THINK I'M SUPPOSED--
WHAT ALIEN MENACE IS THE MARINE CORPS HOLDING AT BAY?
WHAT FORCES YOU TO TAKE AWAY FREEDOM, EVEN LIFE ITSELF?
WHAT DOES THE FACE OF EVIL LOOK LIKE?
LIKE MINE, OKAY?!
LIKE YOURS!
MAKES ME SICK TERRAN REBELS WOULD KILL THEIR OWN KIND-- AND NOT JUST MARINES, BUT CIVILIANS!
SO TODAY I SAVED YOUR LIFE!

YOU'VE GOT *TERRANS* IN THE BRIG...?
NOT ZERG OR PROTOSS, BUT *TERRANS?!*
I-I DON'T KNOW WHAT YOU'RE TALKING ABOUT.
I NEVER SAID THEY WERE TERRANS...
I THINK I BETTER *GO!*
SHOVE
DID HE...
I THINK WE SHOULD SNEAK DOWN TO THE BRIG AND INTERVIEW THE PRISONERS.

I DON'T THINK SO.
HOW CAN YOU BE A REAL REPORTER AND *NOT* GET BOTH SIDES OF THE STORY?!
COME ON!
THEY MYSTERIOUSLY PULL OUT DURING THAT PHONY COLONY TOUR...
...THEN WHEN THEY COME BACK, SUDDENLY THE STORY'S OVER...
...AND WE FIND OUT THE BIG BAD DOMINION MARINES ARE LOCKING UP LITTLE OL' TERRANS?!
YOU SAID WE DIDN'T HAVE A STORY.
WELL, NOW WE DO!
THAT'S *NOT* THE STORY WE'RE HERE TO GET.
YEAH? WELL, MAYBE IT SHOULD BE.
WSSHHT

WHAT DOES THE FACE OF EVIL LOOK LIKE?
LIKE *MINE*, OKAY?!
LIKE *YOURS!*
LIKE *YOURS!*
IS THE CAMERA BATTERY FULLY CHARGED?

DON'T LOOK SUSPICIOUS.
IF WE'RE STOPPED, SAY WE KNOW THE STORY'S OVER...
...WE'RE JUST GETTING PICK-UP SHOTS.
WHAT MADE YOU CHANGE YOUR MIND?
YOU SAID WE SHOULD GET BOTH SIDES OF THE STORY.
I THINK SOME ANGRY REBEL RHETORIC WILL ROUND IT OUT NICELY.
THAT'S NOT WHAT I MEANT.
AND HOW DO YOU KNOW WHERE THE BRIG IS?
LEVEL 1
I DID MY HOMEWORK FOR THIS ASSIGNMENT, WHICH INCLUDED STUDYING THE LAYOUT OF A BATTLECRUISER.
LEVEL 1
BRIG 1
BRIG/1

CAN WE GET SOME LIGHT?
COMING RIGHT UP!
CLICK

CAN I ASK YOU A FEW QUESTIONS?

HEH, KATE LOCKWELL...

WANT ME TO *DANCE* FOR YOU?

DANCE? WHAT DO YOU...?

IF THEY SENT YOU DOWN HERE TO MAKE YOU AND YOUR VIEWERS FEEL BETTER ABOUT YOURSELVES...

...TOO BAD.

MY CAMERAMAN AND I HAD A BET THE BRIG WAS FULL OF TERRAN SCUM.

EASIEST MONEY I EVER MADE.

YOU'RE REALLY GONNA AIR THIS?

IF YOU GIVE ME SOMETHING *NEWSWORTHY*... THEN YEAH, I AM.

WHAT DO YOU MEAN?
I WAS SLEEPIN'!
WHEN THE DOMINION CAME, I WAS SLEEPIN'.
WOKE UP TO A GUN IN MY FACE!
UNN
BUT SURELY YOU WEREN'T SURPRISED?
THE DOMINION MUST DEFEND ITSELF FROM THOSE WHO WOULD HARM ITS CITIZENS!
I AIN'T NO REBEL.
I'M JUST A COLONIST WHO DIDN'T AGREE WITH MY GOVERNMENT.

THE DOMINION ONLY ACTS AGAINST TERRAN REBELS.
THEN WHY HAVE YOU BEEN CAPTURED?
MAYBE TO THEM I AM A REBEL, BUT I NEVER LIFTED A GUN.
I JUST OPENED MY MOUTH.

BECAUSE I DIDN'T RUN.
YOU REALLY WANT SOMETHING "NEWSWORTHY"?
LOOK BEHIND THAT DOOR.
YOUR BIG SCOOP IS IN THERE.

GO GET IT.

KEEP ROLLING...
I AM...
SWIVEL
CHAAANG

BE SURE TO MAKE A HARD COPY.
...
IN FACT, MAKE TWO.

WHAT?

WE'RE GOING TO TAKE A REBEL'S WORD FOR IT?

WE DON'T KNOW WHAT HAPPENED TO THOSE PEOPLE...

TO THOSE *WOMEN AND CHILDREN?*

NO, WE DON'T.

BUT I HAVE A GOOD IDEA WHO MIGHT...

I DON'T KNOW HOW FAR OUT WE ARE...
...BUT MAYBE WE CAN PICK UP MICHAEL LIBERTY'S TRANSMISSION.
LIBERTY'S STILL REPORTING?!
WHAT--DOES HE HAVE AN AUDIENCE OF, LIKE, FIVE PEOPLE?!
REPORTING IS ABOUT A LOT MORE THAN RATINGS, KATE.
HE SWITCHES FREQUENCIES FOR, Y'KNOW, OBVIOUS REASONS...
TXRUWW...WWRRXX...XXRRUWW...
THIS WOULD BE CONSIDERED TREASON, BY THE WAY.
PUNISHABLE BY DEATH.
I SHOULD KNOW.
I DID A STORY ON IT LAST MONTH.
--BELIEVE IT OR NOT, I AM STANDING WHERE THE CANDORE COLONY ONCE STOOD.

A VIBRANT COMMUNITY, THE PEOPLE OF CANDORE-- LIKE MANY OF US-- CAME TO DOUBT THE DOMINION.

AND A FEW OF THEM OFFERED SANCTUARY TO THE INSURGENTS KNOWN AS "THE KNIGHTS OF FREEDOM"...

...THE REBEL GROUP I'M EMBEDDED WITH, WHICH IS HOW I KNOW THAT CANDORE EVER EXISTED.

BUT WHERE IS CANDORE?

THIS PLACE THAT WAS ONCE FULL OF *LIFE* MERE HOURS AGO...

...HAS ***DISAPPEARED*** AS IF IT NEVER EXISTED.

FWOOSH

SO AS NOT TO INSPIRE THOSE WHO NEVER HEARD OF IT...

...AND TO WARN THOSE WHO HAVE.

SIR, I'M PICKING UP AN UNAUTHORIZED TRANSMISSION...

DASH
WSSHHHT
DO NOT MOVE!
I REPEAT! DO NOT MOVE!
GRAB THEIR CAMERA AND COMPUTERS!!
WHAT ARE YOU DOING?!
LET GO OF ME!

BADUM
WSSHHHT
I REVIEWED THE FOOTAGE IN THEIR CAMERA'S MEMORY.
THEY WERE DEFINITELY IN THE BRIG AND... SURROUNDING AREAS.
I ALSO FOUND A HARD COPY OF THEIR EARLIER FOOTAGE, BUT NO HARD COPY OF THE BRIG FOOTAGE.
WHERE'S THE HARD COPY?!

WE DIDN'T GET A CHANCE TO *COPY* IT YET, SIR.
DON'T THROW "SIR" IN MY FACE, YOU LITTLE JERK!
I'VE SEEN YOU THROWING CONDESCENDING LOOKS LEFT AND RIGHT SINCE YOU GOT HERE!
ZACH OLIVER IS *NOT* A REBEL!
THAT UNAUTHORIZED TRANSMISSION--DID THEY BEAM IT OUT OF HERE?
NO--IT WAS AN *INCOMING* TRANSMISSION.
...WAS IT NOW?
GETTING YOUR LATEST ASSIGNMENT, *REBEL?*

DON'T TELL ME YOU'RE THE REBEL, LOCKWELL...?
WHAT?
MAJOR HAWKINS, I AM ONE OF THE DOMINION'S BIGGEST SUPPORTERS!
HOW DO I KNOW THAT WASN'T ALL SOME ACT TO GAIN OUR TRUST?
SO YOU COULD LAND THIS SWEET LITTLE ASSIGNMENT?
YOU ASKED ME TO COME ABOARD, REMEMBER?
YOU'RE RIGHT! YOU'RE RIGHT...WHAT AM I SAYING?
I'M NOT EVEN GOING TO ASK WHY YOU WERE DOWN IN THE BRIG BY YOURSELVES...
BUT IT IS MAKING ME A LITTLE ANTSY THAT YOU'RE LYING ABOUT COPYING THAT FOOTAGE.
BUT I'M NOT LYING.
IT WAS LATE. ZACH WAS GOING TO COPY THE FOOTAGE IN THE MORNING.

STOP!
WHERE ARE WE GOING?!
WHAT IS THAT?!
WHERE ARE YOU PUTTING HIM?!
BEEP
YOU SURE ASK A LOT OF QUESTIONS, LOCKWELL.
I GUESS IT'S YOUR JOURNALISTIC INSTINCTS KICKING IN.
AND I'LL ANSWER YOUR QUESTIONS AS SOON AS YOU ANSWER MINE.
WHERE'S THE HARD COPY?
SHOVE
WAVE

THIS IS AN AIRLOCK.
IF I PUSH THIS BUTTON, IT'LL OPEN THE OTHER SIDE AND SUCK OUT YOUR FRIEND HERE.
INTO *SPACE.*
HE'LL *DIE.*
WHERE'S THE HARD COPY?
THIS IS INSANE!
I...LISTEN, ALL I WANT IS RECORD RATINGS--
AND YOU CAN *STILL* HAVE THEM.
WHERE'S THE HARD COPY?
KATE...!!

WHY'D YOU SNEAK INTO THE BRIG, KATE?!
WHAT MADE YOU DO IT?!
I HAD TO KNOW.
I'VE HAD ENOUGH!!
OPEN
SLAM
EXACTLY.
AND SO DOES EVERYBODY ELSE.

NO...!
YOU MONSTER!
YOU TRAITOR!
YOU SAID YOU BELIEVED IN THE DOMINION!
I DID BELIEVE!
I TRUSTED YOU! I TRUSTED YOU ALL!
HOW COULD I HAVE EVER GUESSED--
--THAT YOU DIDN'T HAVE THE BEST INTENTIONS...?
BECAUSE YOU'RE NOT A VERY GOOD REPORTER, LOCKWELL.

THAT'S--THAT'S NOT TRUE!
AND EVEN IF IT IS...I'M A FAMOUS REPORTER. I'LL BE MISSED.
NOT ONCE EVERYONE FINDS OUT YOU WERE A REBEL SPY.
NOBODY WILL BELIEVE THAT--
YES ,THEY WILL.
WE'LL JUST GET SOME OTHER PATSY REPORTER TO FLOAT THE STORY.
SQUEEZE
BA-ARRUMMBL

WHAT THE HELL?!
THAT BLAST CAME FROM OUTSIDE!!
DASH
MAJOR HAWKINS--?!
TAKE CARE OF IT!
I'M GOING AFTER LOCKWELL!
I'LL BE RIGHT BACK...
...WITH THAT DAMN HARD COPY!
DASH
WSSHHT

TURN
KOOM
CLACK
CLACK

AWW. YOU'RE BREAKING MY HEART, LOCKWELL.
FWUMP
I'M SORRY IF I HURT YOUR FEELINGS.
BUT IT'S NOT LIKE EVERYTHING I SAID WASN'T TRUE.
GO TO HELL.
I SEE YOU HAVE THE HARD COPY.
EXCELLE--
TRTTT
SPLORK
URK!

TRRTT
TRRTT
TRRTT
KA-BAM
ENGAGE!
BAM
ROCK AND ROLL!
KA-BAM
KOOM
TRRTT
KOOM
KOOM
TRRTT
AHH...!

HOLY--!!
YOU'RE KATE LOCKWELL!!
AND YOU'RE...
MICHAEL LIBERTY...

WE'VE GOTTA--
DAMN. I THINK ONE OF YOUR ARTERIES HAS BEEN HIT.

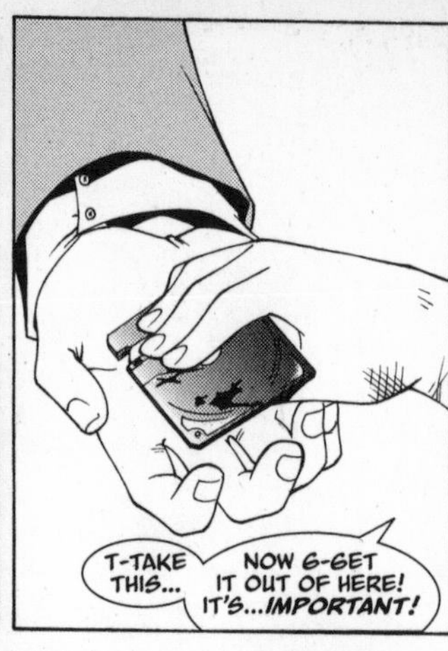

T-TAKE THIS...
NOW G-GET IT OUT OF HERE! IT'S...*IMPORTANT*!

I CAN'T JUST LEAVE YOU HERE, LOCKWELL!

YOU'RE BLEEDING OUT FAST...!

HELP ME GET HER--

NO!!

YOU DON'T UNDERSTAND.
THERE ARE *TWO* COPIES.
THEY NEED TO FIND ME...WITH *THIS* DISK...
...SO THEY WON'T KNOW ABOUT *THAT* DISK...
IF I LEAVE YOU... YOU COULD DIE.
AS LONG AS... THE ST-STORY... DOESN'T DIE...

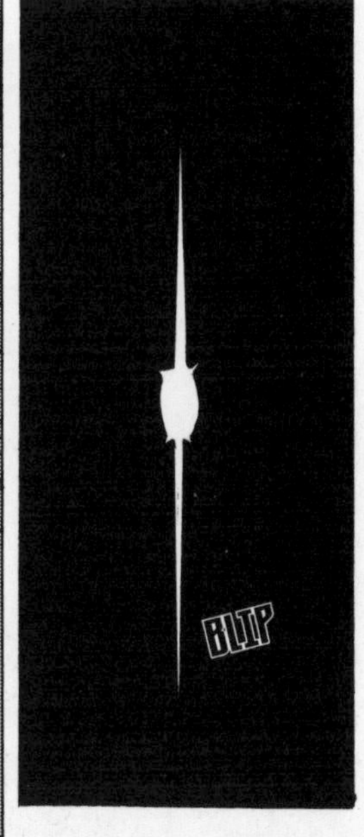

START DOWNLOADING THE FOOTAGE.
AND CHECK THAT DISK...
THINK LOCKWELL DIED ON THE BATTLECRUISER?
JUST CHECK THE DISK.

OKAY, LET'S SEE WHAT SHE GOT...
CAN I ASK YOU A FEW QUESTIONS?
HEH, KATE LOCKWELL...
WANT ME TO DANCE FOR YOU?
FAST-FORWARD.
KEEP ROLLING...
I AM...
STOP!
MY GOD...

LIBERTY! YOU GOTTA SEE THIS!
NOT NOW!
DIDN'T YOU SAY YOU FOUND KATE LOCKWELL ON THAT BATTLECRUISER?
YEAH...
WELL SHE'S ON TV...
THIS IS A UNN SPECIAL REPORT!
WE TAKE YOU LIVE TO THE BATTLECRUISER VICTORY WHERE KATE LOCKWELL REPORTS!
KATE?
THANK YOU, TOM!
I CAME ABOARD TO SEE WHAT LIFE IS LIKE FOR OUR BRAVE DOMINION MARINES--
--AND I CAME FACE-TO-FACE WITH THE HARSH REALITY WHEN WE WERE ATTACKED BY REBELS.
UNN

AND THE REBELS SHOWED NO MERCY.
MAJOR TOM HAWKINS WAS GUNNED DOWN DEFENDING THE SHIP...
...WHILE EVERY SINGLE COLONIST THE MARINES WERE TAKING TO A SAFE-HAVEN WAS MURDERED.
WHAT A HACK...
WHAT THE HELL HAPPENED?

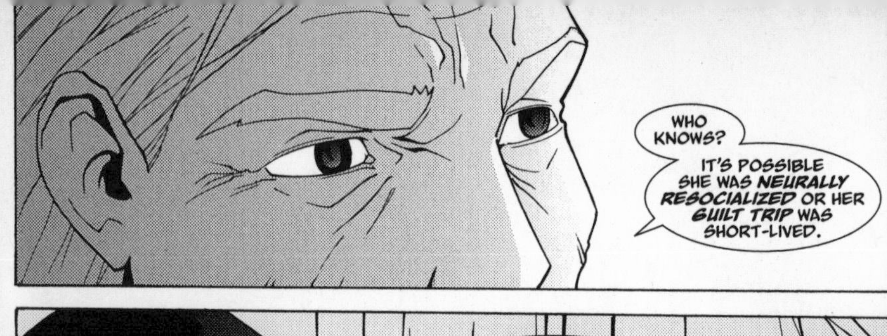
WHO KNOWS?
IT'S POSSIBLE SHE WAS NEURALLY RESOCIALIZED OR HER GUILT TRIP WAS SHORT-LIVED.

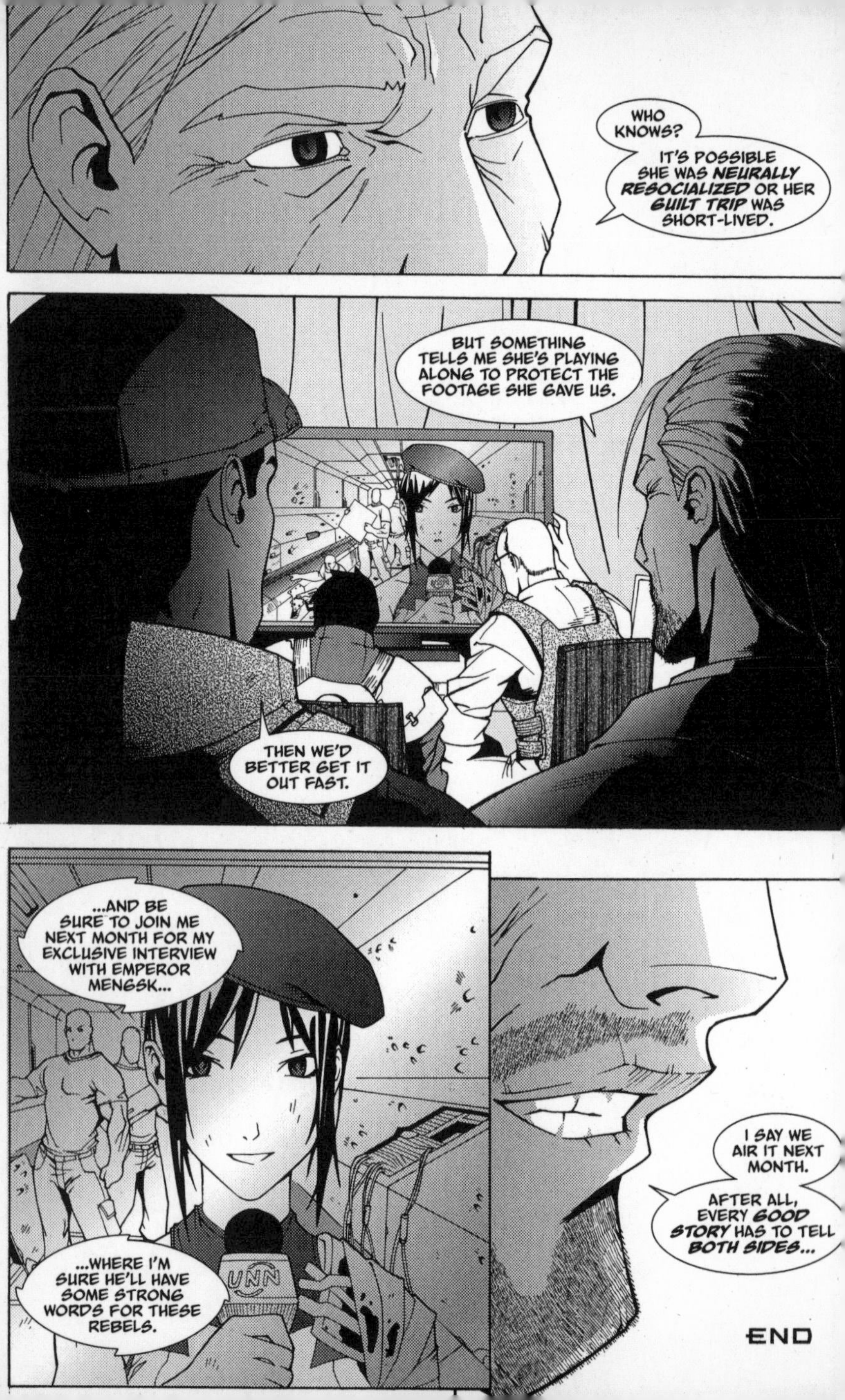

BUT SOMETHING TELLS ME SHE'S PLAYING ALONG TO PROTECT THE FOOTAGE SHE GAVE US.
THEN WE'D BETTER GET IT OUT FAST.
...AND BE SURE TO JOIN ME NEXT MONTH FOR MY EXCLUSIVE INTERVIEW WITH EMPEROR MENGSK...
...WHERE I'M SURE HE'LL HAVE SOME STRONG WORDS FOR THESE REBELS.
UNN
I SAY WE AIR IT NEXT MONTH.
AFTER ALL, EVERY GOOD STORY HAS TO TELL BOTH SIDES...
END

StarCraft

Frontline

Volume 2

A Ghost Story

Written by Kieron Gillen

Art by Hector Sevilla

Letterer: Michael Paolilli

KEL-MORIAN SALVAGE VESSEL
34-C: "THE GENEROUS PROFIT"

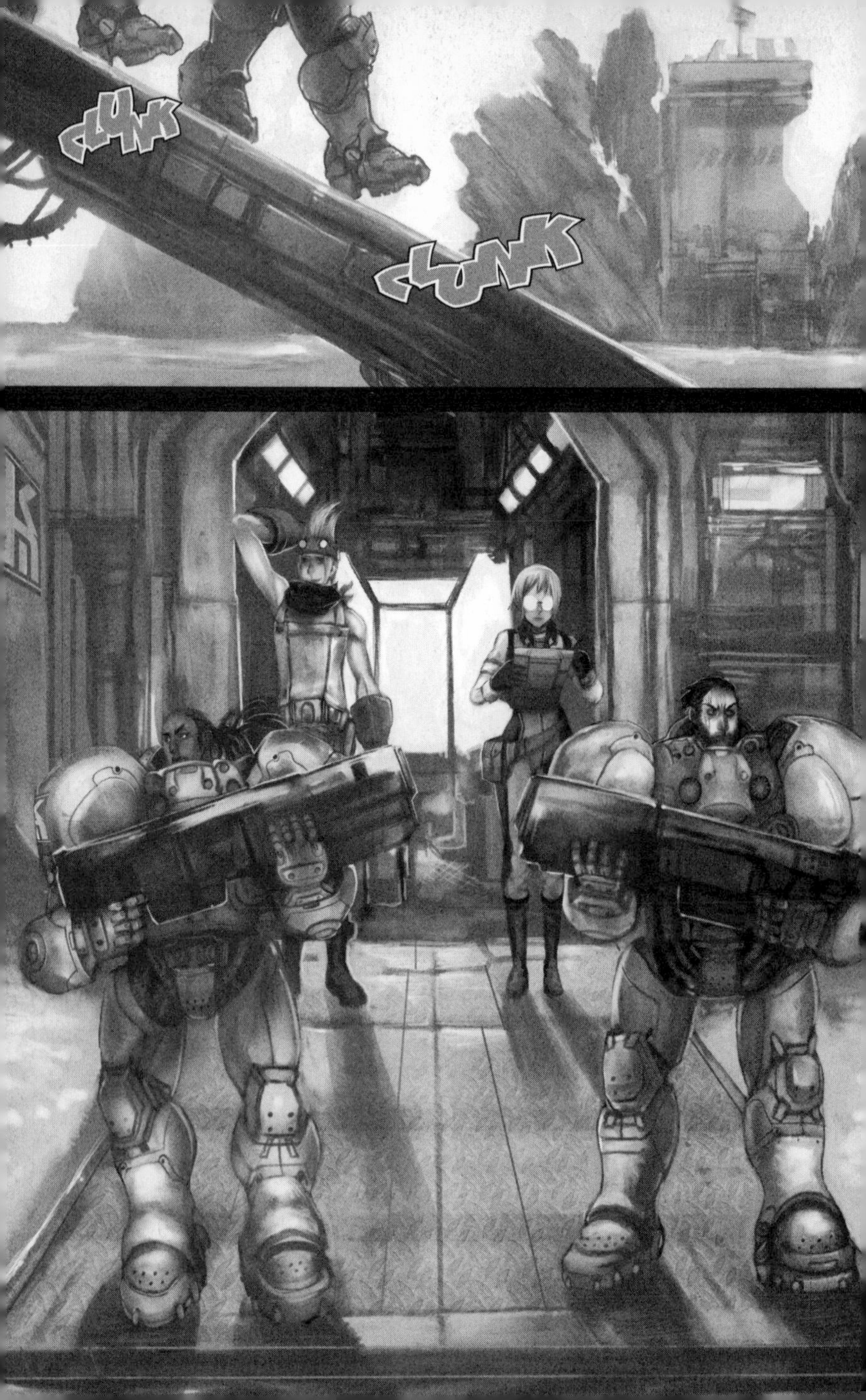

CLUNK
CLUNK

WHERE ARE WE AGAIN?
IS THIS THE PROMISED LAND OF SILK AND MONEY?
SHUT UP. YOU KNOW WHAT IT IS.
IT'S A ROCK IN THE MIDDLE OF NOWHERE.
ACTUALLY, SIR, IT'S A STANDARD-6 FRINGE WORLD WITH A FERROUS CORE AND--
I KNOW. *SHUT UP.*
ROCK.
LUKE KEEGAN: ENGINEER
URIAH CYRIS: SALVAGE COMMANDER
MACY CLIFT: INFORMATION OFFICER
CHUCK TYROSINE: COMBAT SPECIALIST

ANY CHANCE OF THERE BEING SOMETHING WORTH ACTUAL REAL CREDITS THIS TIME, MACY?
IT BETTER NOT BE. FOR ALL OUR SAKES.
SIR, I STRONGLY OBJECT TO THIS CONTINUED INSINUATION OF BLAME FOR OUR CONTINUING PREDICAMENT.
YOU'RE THE INFORMATION OFFICER.
WHEN WE KEEP ON ENDING UP ON ROCKS WITHOUT ENOUGH SALVAGE TO BUY A DECENT SANDWICH, WHO AM I SUPPOSED TO BLAME?!
CHUCK?!

HEY, CHUCK--WHY DID YOU TAKE US ON A DRY SPELL SO LONG THAT WE CAN'T EVEN PAY FOR THIS MONTH'S COMMISSION?!
IT'S ALWAYS PROBABILITIES, SIR.
WE'VE BEEN INCREDIBLY UNFORTUNATE.
TRUST ME.
YOU DON'T KNOW HOW "UNFORTUNATE" UNFORTUNATE CAN GET.
IF I END UP LOSING THE SHIP, YOU'RE GOING TO END UP AS...
A SAVAGE SALVAGE QUEEN IN A REALM OF ROCKS?
LUKE! JUST SHUT UP, AND GO TO WORK!

WE NEED THIS HOLE IN THE GROUND OPENED UP.
SURE THING, BOSS.
ZAK
SHUK
ANY IDEA WHAT KINDA PLACE IT IS?
JUST ANOTHER ABANDONED STRUCTURE.
MINERS, PROBABLY.
NO POWER SIGNALS.
I *SAID* IT WAS ABANDONED.
PROBABLY LEFT WHEN A SEAM PROVED DRY.

BEWARE
YOU
About Our People

FLIK

CARE TO REVISE THAT OPINION, BOSS?

SHUT UP.

ANY SIGNALS?

VVRZZZ

BZZK

NO, SIR. NOT A THING.

WHOEVER DID THIS IS LONG GONE.

BARE BONES KIND OF TOLD ME THAT, MACY.

SOMEONE IS GOING TO SUE THIS BESAINTED PELAGIUS GUY OVER THAT "PROTECTS YOU" THING.

KNOCK IT OFF. WE SWEEP THE BASE.

LET'S SEE IF THERE'S ANYTHING WORTH TAKING.

LOOKS LIKE THE GENERATOR.

WANT ME TO TURN IT ON?

DO IT.
WELL, I'LL HAVE TO ***DRESS UP PRETTY*** AND ***FLIRT*** A LITTLE.

JUST ***DO IT,*** YOU PERVERT.
WE'LL FIND OPS.

MACY?

IT'S A CUSTOMIZED **MARK 2 SYSTEM.**

HEAVILY UPGRADED. CUSTOMIZED TECH.

I'D GUESS BIOMECHANICAL RESEARCH, SYSTEMIC CALCULATION--

I DON'T NEED THE SCIENCE. JUST GIVE ME ANSWERS.
CAN YOU ACCESS IT?

...NO.
WHY NOT?

NO POWER.
ONE DAY I'M GOING TO FIRE YOU MACY, AND IT'LL BE A HAPPY DAY INDEED.
LUKE? PROGRESS ON THE GENERATOR?

JUST ABOUT TO FLIP THE SWITCH NOW, MY CAPTAIN.
VZZZT
ZZZRT
ZZZT
AND LET THERE BE...
...LIGHT.
LOADING...
WELL DONE, LUKE.
YOU DIDN'T MAKE A HASH OF IT.
MACY?

HUH?
WE HAVE FILES. HEAVY ENCRYPTION. DEMARCATED INTERNALLY.
CLAK
CLAK
SEGMENTED, LIKE A SHIP. INTERNAL AIRLOCKS AND BRIDGEHEADS SO THE WHOLE THING DOESN'T CRACK AT ONCE.
STARTING
I HAVE TO TAKE IT DOWN ONE SEGMENT AT A TIME.
GET TO IT, THEN.
ALREADY HAVE, SIR.
FIRST BLOCK DOWN.
CLAKKA
CLAKKA
CLK CLK
...IN PROGRESS...
CLAKKA CLA-
!
LOADING...

ANY OF THIS CULT'S BABBLE LOOK LIKE IT'S WORTH ANYTHING?
...
MACY!
THIS PELAGIUS WAS A SCIENTIST. HIS WORK WAS...
IT'S HYBRID CHEM/BIO/NEURO-RESEARCH POINTING TOWARDS A SYNERGETIC APPROACH TOWARDS...
...OH, THIS IS AMAZING!
URIAH
STOP TALKING SCIENCE AT ME.
HOW MUCH IS IT WORTH?
IT'S BEYOND CUTTING EDGE RESEARCH.
I CAN'T EVEN BEGIN TO GUESS.
URIAH
YOU BEGIN BY MAKING A COPY.
OH--GOT A LOG ENTRY.
PLAYING.
CLAKKA

FILE 0067
RECORD OF THE CHURCH OF BESAINTED PELAGIUS--BROTHER 2 SPEAKING.
RECORD OF THE BESAINTED CHURCH
RECORDING
THIS MOST-BLESSED COLONY CONTINUES IN HAPPINESS, AS IS ONLY RIGHT IN THE PRESENCE OF HIS ETERNAL GENIUS.
EVEN THE CURIOUS DEATHS OF BROTHERS 4 AND 7 FAZE US NOT.
THOUGH BROTHERS IN THE LESSER NUMBERS HAVE CONFESSED THAT THE SCREAMS OF BROTHER 4 WERE SOMEWHAT... DISTURBING.
RECORDING...
ARRRGGGGHHHH!

LOCKED
SLAM
DOOR'S SEALED.
WELL, GET IT OPEN, MACY!
LUKE!
ANSWER ME, YOU DAMNED IDIOT!
YOU BETTER NOT BE PLAYING AROUND!

H-HERE...
SOMETHING'S OUT HERE!
HUFF HUFF

WHAT IS IT, MAN?!
WHAT CAN YOU SEE?!
I'M AT THE BULKHEAD!
OPEN IT!
HUFF HUFF
PROTECTS YOU
MACY'S ON IT! HOLD ON!
THUD
SLUMP
NO!
NO!
NO!
OPEN IT!
PLEASE! OPEN IT NOW!
OPEN IT, MACY!
GOT IT, I'VE GOT IT...!
VSHHH
OPEN

WOOOSH
PELAGIOUS
PROTECTS YOU

MACY. READING ANYTHING?
N...NO, SIR.
LOADING...
HOW LONG WILL IT TAKE TO DECRYPT THE REST OF THE INFORMATION?
I'LL ESTIMATE FULL D-DECRYPTION WILL B-BE...TWO HOURS?
TWO HOURS...

OKAY. CHUCK--
COMBAT READY.
SWEEP THE
BASE.
KEEP IN
CONTACT.
TAK
TAK
TAK
TAK
MACY, PASS ME
THE SCANNER.
I'LL KEEP
WATCH FOR
MOVEMENT.
YOU GET
CRACKING.
WE'RE HERE TO
DO A JOB.
AFFIRMATIVE,
SIR.
A JOB THAT
BETTER MAKE
US RICH.

PROGRESS?
GETTING THERE, SIR.
LOGS ARE LEAKING OUT. SEEMS TO BE CHRONOLOGICALLY.
TAK
TAK
PLAY 'EM AS YOU GET 'EM.
RECORD OF
RECORDI
FILE 0069
THE DEATHS CONTINUE, BUT DON'T AFFECT THE JOY WITH WHICH WE APPROACH OUR DAILY WORK.
OUR DAILY WORK INCLUDES *SEARCHING!*
AND CREATING *BARRICADES!*
RECORD OF
RECORDING
FILE 0069
WE ARE... *INEFFECTIVE.*

RECORDING...
BROTHERS 8 AND 9 ARE GONE!
WE FOUND BROTHER 5 SCREAMING.
SAID AN ANGEL CAME FOR HIM.
HE DIED BEFORE WE COULD STOP THE BLEEDING.
RECORDING...
BESAINTED BROTHER PELAGIUS THE FIRST CLAIMS HIS SUPREME WATCHMAKER-GIFTED SCIENCE WILL PROTECT US.
BUT THE LESSER BROTHERS ARE SPEAKING OF NOISES IN THE NIGHT...
GHOSTS WHISPERING...
OM OM OM OM OM
OM OM OM OM OM OM OM

ILE 0076

OM OM OM OM OM OM

HA HA HA HA

RECORD OF THE BESAINTED CHURCH...

FILE 0076

RECORDIN

I HEAR THEM, TOO.

THIS IS A TIME OF... *TESTING.*

OM OM OM OM OM

OM OM OM OM OM OM OM

HA HA HA HA

HA HA HA HA

STOMP STOMP STOMP

THE PEOPLE HERE WERE BEING PICKED OFF, ONE BY ONE.

THEY THOUGHT THEY WERE BEING HAUNTED.

THEY HEARD VOICES, TOO...

LEAVE.
CHUCK, I HAVEN'T TIME FOR THIS. MORE WORDS. GIVE ME MORE *WORDS*.
YOU CAN BORROW SOME OF MACY'S.
SHE'S GOT PLENTY.
US.
LEAVE.

THERE'S A CHANCE OF PROTOSS INTERFERENCE HERE AND...
...CAPTAIN, WHILE I DON'T BELIEVE IN THE SUPERNATURAL...
...WELL, IT'S POSSIBLE THAT THERE'S A PREVIOUSLY UNKNOWN MALIGN ALIEN ENTITY WHICH FEEDS OFF THE PSYCHIC ENERGY OF THE DEATHS OF THIS PLACE, AND HAS INCARNATED TO...
WELL, IT'S AN EARLY HYPOTHESIS. I CONCUR WITH CHUCK.
WE SHOULD LEAVE. NOW.
STOP IT!!
THE PAIR OF YOU!!
RIAH

THINK HOW MUCH THAT INFORMATION IS WORTH!
THIS IS WHAT WE'VE ALL DREAMED OF!
THIS DOESN'T JUST DIG US OUT OF THE HOLE--THIS SETS US UP FOR *LIFE.*
I'VE SPENT TWENTY YEARS TALKING ABOUT THAT *ONE BIG SCORE.*
THIS IS IT. FORGET THE COMMISSION. SELL THIS TO THE HIGHEST BIDDER, AND WE'LL NEVER HAVE TO WORK AGAIN!
PULL YOURSELVES TOGETHER. STAY HERE AND STAY CALM.
I'LL SEARCH FOR LUKE.
TAK
TAK
JUST REMEMBER, THERE'S *NO SUCH THING...*

...AS GHOS--
KA-ZLCHHHHHH
GLURRAAGH!!

VRRTT
GURGGLE
VRRTT
VRRTT
WOSHH
VRRTT
BAM
LOCKED
GET DATA.

ARE YOU DERANGED, CHUCK?!
WE NEED TO GO!!
WE NEED TO GO NOW!!
ONLY ONE WAY OUT. PROBABLY DEAD IF WE LEAVE NOW, TOO.
IF WE GET OUT, SHIP'S COMMISSION'S OURS.
IF WE CAN PAY FOR IT.
BE GOOD TO NOT HAVE TO WORK FOR SOMEONE LIKE URIAH AGAIN.

OKAY, OKAY... I'LL FINISH!

JUST WATCH MY BACK, YEAH?

MY LIFE'S ALWAYS BEEN ABOUT PROBABILITIES.

RISK AND ***REWARD.***

AND I'LL TELL YOU THIS, CHUCK...

FOR THE CHANCE OF NEVER HAVING TO ANSWER TO AN ASS LIKE URIAH AGAIN... IT'S GOT TO BE ***WORTH*** THE ***RISK.***

WHIRR
WHIRR
OM OM OM OM
RECORDING...
MORE DEATHS. ONLY PELAGIUS AND I REMAIN OF THE HIGH BROTHERS.
THE LESSER NUMBERS SEARCH. THEY FIND NOTHING.
PELAGIUS' SOOTHING WORDS ARE NOT ENOUGH. THE CHILDREN ARE SCREAMING...
FILE 0112
OM OM OM OM
DO YOU HEAR THAT?
OM OM OM OM
RECORDING...
BESAINTED PELAGIUS IS AT WORK ON A GREAT MACHINE TO TRAP THIS INTRUDER. HE CLAIMS IT WILL ALL BE OVER SOON.
WE TRY TO HAVE FAITH.
OM OM OM OM

HA HA HA HA HA HA
CHUCK? I ASKED IF YOU *HEARD* THAT?
ARE THESE THE ***END TIME*** HE PROPHESIE
WE FEAR SO.
HE SAID WE ALONE WOULD SURVIVE... BUT IT SEEMS WE WILL ALSO ***PERISH***.
WE WILL BE AMONG THE ***PURGED***.
DIDN'T USED TO BELIEVE IN GHOSTS.
DO NOW.

HEH.
DIRECT EXPERIENCE *DOES* HAVE A TENDENCY TO UNDERMINE SEEMINGLY STRONG THEORETICAL POSITIONS.
AND... *YES!*
OKAY. GOT IT. DOWNLOADING NOW.

CHUCK, I WISH YOU'D TALK MORE.
CONVERSATION'S THERAPEUTIC EFFECT ON THE NERVOUS SYSTEM IS WELL ESTABLISHED.

THE BESAINTED CHUR

NO. NO.
THIS IS INSANE!! IT CAN'T BE A GHOST!!
BLIP
GOOD NEWS!
THE BROTHERS REJOICE!
THE BESAINTED CHURCH
RECORDI
THE BESAINTED PELAGIUS' GLORIOUS MACHINE SAVED US! WE HAVE FOUND THE INTRUDER.
IT WAS A STEALTH AGENT SENT BY THE CONFEDERACY TO BRING US TO AN END!
WE HAVE CAPTURED THE HERETIC! BROTHER PELAGIUS CLAIMS THAT HE CAN--THROUGH THE DIVINE INSPIRATION OF THE SUPREME WATCHMAKER--TURN THIS "GHOST."
A NEW AND MOST PUISSANT BROTHER!
REJOICE! REJOICE!

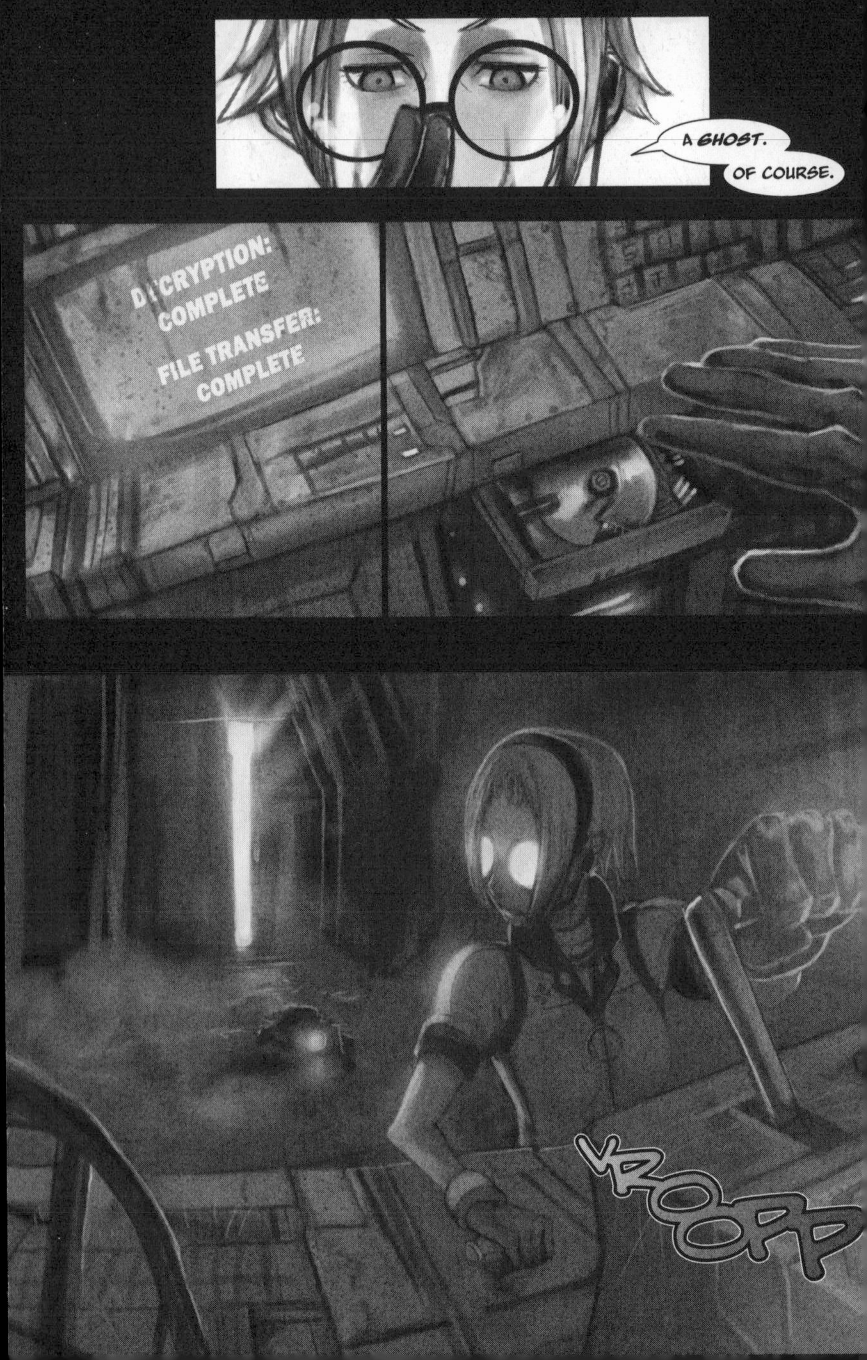

A GHOST.
OF COURSE.
DECRYPTION:
COMPLETE
FILE TRANSFER:
COMPLETE
VROOPP

BEWARE
HUFF
HUFF
HUFF
HUFF
HUFF
HUFF
HUFF
HUUUAGH!

HUFF

THRUSSHT

GOOD DAY, CHILD.

HE'LL PILOT IT AWAY FROM THIS PLACE, AND THEN HE'LL EJECT. WE DON'T WANT THE KEL-MORIANS KNOWING EXACTLY WHERE YOU WENT MISSING.
OUR PRIVACY IS AN IMPORTANT THING, YOU UNDERSTAND.
IT WAS THE ARRIVAL OF OUR GHOST BROTHER THAT TAUGHT ME PRIVACY'S IMPORTANCE.
IT REVEALED THE CONFEDERACY, NOT UNDERSTANDING MY CLOSENESS TO DIVINITY, WAS GROWING PARANOID.
THEY FEARED THE KNOWLEDGE THE SUPREME WATCHMAKER GIFTED ME. THEY FEARED MY EVER-GROWING FLOCK.
THEY WOULD STEAL MY HOLY SECRETS AND KILL US WITH THEIR PETTY HATE.
AFTER WE CAPTURED AND TURNED OUR GHOST BROTHER, WE HID, EVEN DEEPER.
ISN'T THAT RIGHT, MY CHILDREN?

YES, BESAINTED FATHER.
THE CHILDREN'S LAUGHTER...*WAS* FROM CHILDREN.
A LOWER LEVEL.
MY, YOU'RE SMART.
FOR AN UNBELIEVER.
YOU'RE HIDING...FROM THE CONFEDERACY? BUT THEY'VE BEEN FINISHED FOR YEARS.
WHY...?
I KNEW OF THEIR FALL, BUT THEY WERE ALWAYS THE LEAST OF MY PROBLEMS.
AND THE NATURE OF THEIR FAILURE CONFIRMED MY GRAND VISION.

MAR SARA. ANTIGA PRIME. CHAU SARA.
CLEANSED BY A SEARING LIGHT FROM ALIEN GODS.
AS I PROPHESIED-- A GREAT BURNING, TO CAUTERIZE THE UNIVERSE.
IT WILL SPARE *ONLY* US.
SO WE REMAIN HERE, AND CONTINUE OUR WORK, UNTIL THE LIGHT FINISHES ITS. IN A DECADE, THERE WILL BE NO LIFE LEFT, BARRING US BROTHERS.
AND THE *UNIVERSE* WILL BE OURS.
S-SO...ARE YOU GOING TO KILL ME LIKE THE REST?
NO... WE WON'T KILL YOU.
NO NEED.

UNLIKE THOSE MILITARY MEN, YOU ARE NOT A FIGHTER.

YOU'LL *JOIN US*. ANOTHER *FAITHFUL BELIEVER*.

YOU'RE INSANE!

OH, YOU'LL JOIN. YOU'LL FIND I'M... *VERY* PERSUASIVE.

AREN'T I, BROTHER 651?

YES, BESAINTED PELAGIUS.

LUKE...!

OUR GHOST BROTHER'S NEURAL INHIBITOR WAS AN INSPIRATION.
A DEVICE TO SHAPE HIS WILL TO HIS MASTERS' LIKING.
MY TEACHINGS AND METHODS GATHERED MANY TO MY FLOCK-- BUT WHY RISK FICKLE HUMAN MINDS?
MY TECHNOLOGY HAS ALWAYS BEEN HOLY. MY CREATIONS, THE SUPREME WATCHMAKER'S TEMPORAL PRESENCE.
SO WHY NOT INSTALL AN UNBREAKING MECHANICAL FAITH INTO THE BROTHERS?
IT ISN'T A BAD THING, MACY.
MY MIND IS FULL OF LIGHT.
COME WITH US, BROTHER 652!
BROTHER 652!

END

SIMON FURMAN

Simon Furman is a writer for comic books and TV animation, his name inextricably linked to ***Transformers***, the 80s toy phenomenon. He has written for ***Transformers: Infiltration/Escalation/Devastation, Beast Wars: The Gathering/The Ascending, Transformers: Spotlight*** and ***Transformers UK***. Other comic book credits include ***Dragon's Claws, Death's Head, Alpha Flight, Turok, She-Hulk, Robocop*** and ***What If?*** In the TV animation field, Furman has written for shows such as ***Beast Wars, Roswell Conspiracies, Dan Dare, X-Men: Evolution, Alien Racers*** and ***A.T.O.M.*** Furman's recent/current writing work includes ***Terminator 2 — Infinity, Ronan, Death's Head 3.0, Teenage Mutant Ninja Turtles,*** and ***Torchwood***. He is also the author of ***Transformers: The Ultimate Guide,*** a lavish twentieth anniversary hardcover, ***You Can Draw Transformers*** and a ***Doctor Who*** audio adventure (The Axis of Insanity).

GRACE RANDOLPH

Grace Randolph is a comedic actor and writer born and raised in New York City. Previously she's written ***Justice League Unlimited #41*** for DC Comics and ***Nemesis: Who Me?*** for TOKYOPOP's Pilot Program. Her upcoming work is an adaptation of Meg Cabot's Jinx for manga, as well as the continuation of her ***Warcraft: Legends*** Volume 2 story "Warrior: Divided" in ***Warcraft: Legends*** Volume 5. Outside of comics, Grace is the host/writer/producer of the webshow ***RevYOU***, which can be seen on YouTube and NBC/Bravo's ***Television Without Pity*** website. Grace also studies at the Upright Citizens Brigade Theatre (UCB) where she has written, performed and produced the shows "Situation: Awkward" and "Igor On Strike." Visit her informative—and awesome!—website at www.gracerandolph.com.

KIERON GILLEN

Kieron Gillen splits his life between being an award-winning journalist and a critically-acclaimed comic writer. His breakthrough work was ***Phonogram: Rue Britannia*** for Image comics, which Warren Ellis described as "one of the few truly essential comics of 2006." His other comics works include ***newuniversal: 1959*** for Marvel Comics and ***Warhammer: Crown of Destruction*** for Boom. He's currently at work preparing an ongoing series for ***Avatar*** in which he plans to have a bit too much fun, and is preparing for the return of ***Phonogram*** in December 2008. He is an easy victim for even the most inexpert zerg rushes. Don't hurt him.

ARTISTS:

ESSE ELLIOTT

esse Elliott was born in S. Korea, but has lived most of his life in New Orleans, LA. e began drawing at a very young age and started collecting comic books as a child, which further fueled his interest in art. He discovered anime and manga while attending college at the University of New Orleans, where he received a degree in Fine Arts. pon graduating, Jesse spent many successful years as the manager of a video-game store, but left to pursue a career in illustration. More of his work can be seen online at jelli76.deviantart.com.

TOMÁS AIRA

omás Aira was born and lives in Buenos Aires, Argentina. He has studied the arts and comic techniques since childhood and began publishing in a variety of local magazines and books, eventually achieving publication of his finest work, the graphic novel ***78 mp/h*** (soon to be published in the US). Tomas is a key member of Altercomics Studios. e also illustrates the horror miniseries ***Night & Fog*** for Studio 407, and is the current artist for the highly-acclaimed webseries ***Marilith*** at www.marilith.com. This is his first major assignment for Blizzard/TOKYOPOP.

NAM KIM

lam Kim made his manga debut with the TOKYOPOP Star Trek short "The Trial," which appeared in TOKYOPOP's ***Star Trek: the manga - Kakan ni Shinkou***, and his Blizzard debut with "An Honest Trade" in ***Warcraft: Legends*** Volume 1. He is the creator of OKYOPOP's upcoming science-fiction/fantasy epic ***Adomant***.

HECTOR SEVILLA

lector Sevilla hails from Chihuahua, Mexico. He is a huge fan of ***StarCraft***, and never magined he would ever help create a part of the ***StarCraft*** universe. He thanks Kathy Schilling, Paul Morrissey and Blizzard for the wonderful opportunity. In addition o creating ***Lullaby*** and working on ***Leviticus Cross*** and Konami's ***Lunar Knights***, Hector s developing a new property called ***DrawSkill*** for TOKYOPOP's Pilot Program. You can ake a sneak peek at ***DrawSkill*** at http://elsevilla.deviantart.com

The seed of a great idea—to create more ***StarCraft*** stories—soaked up fan support, spread its branches and sprouted into the hearty tree of ***StarCraft: Frontline 2***. I hope you've enjoyed sinking your teeth into the very freshest and finest in ***StarCraft*** content this tree has borne.

Thanks goes to previous contributors Simon Furman, Jesse Elliott and Hector Sevilla, who sheltered their editor through the tumultuous world of ***StarCraft*** and the frenetic ***Frontline*** storms. No one on the team could be called a true seedling; Nam Kim and Grace Randolph brought expertise from their work on ***Warcraft: Legends***, and Kieron Gillen and Tomàs Aira each have years of comic experience under their belts. Also thanks to resident ***StarCraft*** expert Michael Paolilli and to editor extraodinaire Troy Lewter... a man who can see the forest **and** the trees.

But none of that dedication and talent would have taken root without Blizzard. At every opportunity, the Blizzard staff extended its wisdom, guidance and passion. I'd like to thank our immediate pillars of support at Blizzard—Jason Bischoff, Micky Neilson, Rob Tokar and Evelyn Fredericksen— for their ongoing nurturing of ***Frontline***. Without their guiding hands, the ***Frontline*** series surely would not have become the heir to the ***StarCraft*** empire it's become. And of course, a big thanks goes out to the top man himself, Chris Metzen--who's still contributing that Jim Raynor story to volume 4, by the way!

That's right, volume 4. Thanks to the support of all you dedicated fans and to the series' overwhelming popularity and success, we've added another volume of ***Frontline***. That means more explosions, more intrigue, and best of all, more tie-ins to future TOKYOPOP ***StarCraft*** manga such as ***Ghost Academy*** by Keith R. A. DeCandido!

Here at the close of volume 2, I'm reminded of the old adage, because it rings true—"Grow old along with me, the best is yet to be."

Hope Donovan
Editor

StarCraft

Frontline™

In The Next Volume...

You've just read four tales of haunting, abomination, deceit and fear... but still you look toward the future, fixing your eyes upon further *StarCraft* adventures that await you on the near horizon...

The sadistic Dr. Burgess, from volume one's "Why We Fight," gets his bloody hands on Muadun, a recently captured protoss High Templar...

A lounge singer on a backwater planet brokers an unlikely peace between the Kel-Morians and the Dominion, until the zerg arrive...

To save her race after the zerg attack on Aiur, a protoss teacher learns to embrace the fearsome powers of the dark...

Senator Phash's innocent young son from volume one's "Weapon of War," is hunted by a government that would turn him into a killer...

So suit up in your marine armor, get on the FRONTLINE, and prepare yourself for another intense barrage of *StarCraft* stories!

STARCRAFT:
FRONTLINE VOLUME 3

COMING JULY 2009

SNEAK PEEK

Now that you have battled amongst the stars, it's time to head for the untamed lands of Azeroth and experience the thrilling fantasy-adventure that is *Warcraft: Legends.* TOKYOPOP is thrilled to present this series of anthologies based on Warcraft, Blizzard's global MMORPG phenomenon. On the next page you'll find a sneak peak of "Family Values," one of the four stories featured in *Warcraft: Legends Volume 2.*

A relentlessly savage story of redemption written by Aaron Sparrow and drawn by In-Bae Kim, "Family Values" is the story of a noble orc caught in the middle of the slaughter of Draenor's draenei--a campaign of bloodlust led by his own brother, J'argg. Jaruk suffers in silence as the draenei body count grows around him...but when he is unexpectedly placed into the role of protector, he is thrust into a battle that pits brother against brother...

Warcraft: Legends Volume 2 is available now!

Draenor--One year before the First War between orcs and humans
CUT THEM DOWN!!
LEAVE NONE ALIVE!!
HUFF... HUFF... HUFF...
EH...?
AAH!!

*⟨QUICKLY, BOY, YOU MUST RU--⟩
YAAAAAH!!
*⟨I'LL MAKE YOU PAY, MONSTER...!⟩
UNNGHF!!
THUD
*TRANSLATED FROM THE DRAENEI TONGUE
⟨KILL YOU FOR WHAT YOU'VE--⟩
⟨DO IT.⟩
⟨WHAT? I... YOUR EYES...⟩
⟨THE OTHERS... THEIR EYES GLOW RED LIKE EMBERS OF A DYING FIRE...
BUT YOURS DO NOT...!⟩
⟨I SAID DO IT, BOY! AVENGE YOUR FAMILY!⟩
⟨DO IT NOW!!⟩
⟨I...I...⟩

SQUEALCH

YOU MUST BE RUSTY, ALLOWING A **MANGY CUR** LIKE THIS TO GET THE BETTER OF YOU.

FORGIVE ME, J'ARGG.
PERHAPS KILLING **WOMEN** AND **CHILDREN** ON THESE RAIDS HAS SLOWED MY HAND.

OR **PERHAPS** IF YOU WIELDED YOUR **AXE** AS EXPERTLY AS YOU DO YOUR **TONGUE** I WOULDN'T HAVE HAD TO COME TO YOUR AID!

NOW TAKE UP YOUR WEAPON AND GET TO THE TASK AT HAND!

I KNOW YOUR HEART BURNS FOR GREATER SPORT, JARUK...AS DOES MINE.

WE MAY YET FIND IT, AND PERHAPS IN GLORIOUS BATTLE YOU MIGHT REKINDLE YOUR CONNECTION TO THE ELEMENTS. BUT UNTIL THEN...

SHHHHNK
...WE WILL EXTERMINATE THESE DRAENEI VERMIN, AS GUL'DAN COMMANDS!
CAPTAIN!
WE HAVE FOUND ANOTHER GROUP OF REFUGEES...!
ANY MALES AMONG THEIR NUMBER?
THEY ARE ENCAMPED IN THE CLIFFS AHEAD!
I COUNTED TEN THAT LOOK TO BE ABLE FIGHTERS!
THERE IS YOUR SPORT, JARUK!
CUT THEM DOWN WHERE THEY STAND!!

MY NAME IS **JARUK BLOODFYRE** OF THE SHADOWMOON CLAN.
I AM AN ORC.
ALTHOUGH, TRUTH BE TOLD, I KNOW NOT WHAT THAT MEANS ANYMORE.
GUL'DAN AND HIS DARK ALLIANCE WITH DEMONS HAVE TWISTED MY ONCE NOBLE CLAN INTO SOMETHING **BLOODTHIRSTY** AND **SAVAGE**.
UNLIKE MY BROTHER, I DID **NOT DRINK** FROM THE **CHALICE OF REBIRTH**.
I ASK THE ELEMENTS WHO NO LONGER ANSWER... DOES THAT MAKE ME LESS CULPABLE FOR THIS MADNESS...OR **MORE**?
I AM...**WAS**...A SHAMAN.
AS A SHAMAN, IT WAS MY DUTY TO FIRST SEEK A PEACEFUL RESOLUTION BEFORE UNLEASHING THE WRATH OF THE ELEMENTS UPON MY ENEMIES.
I LOOKED UPON THE AXE AS A BLUNT INSTRUMENT, AN UNWIELDY, **GRUESOME** WEAPON OF WAR...
...BUT NOW MY BROTHER HAS RECENTLY FORCED ME TO CARRY ONE, THOUGH IT IS AS **INEFFECTIVE** IN MY UNSKILLED HANDS AS A **NEWBORN'S RATTLE**.

I ONCE SHUNNED THE PATH OF VIOLENCE.

WHICH IS WHY I SOMETIMES WONDER...

THUNK

THUNK

...WHEN I BECAME SO **ADEPT** AT IT.

PANT...HUFF... PANT...

BLOOD...ON MY HANDS...

BY THE ANCIENT ELEMENTS...WHAT HAVE WE BECOME?!

HA!! THAT'S THE *SPIRIT*, BROTHER!
H-HAVE TO ESCAPE THIS MADNESS... HAVE TO TH-THINK...
THERE... THAT CAVERN...

<PLEASE, ALIUS, COME WITH US!>
<I CANNOT, MY LOVE! I WOULD ONLY SLOW YOU DOWN.>
<AT LEAST THIS WAY, I CAN BUY YOU AND LEENA TIME TO ESCAPE...!>

<I WON'T LEAVE YOU!>
<DADDY!>
<YOU MUST!>
<IF I AM ABLE, I *WILL* FIND YOU...! I LOVE Y-->

‹GO!›
‹NOW!!›
‹WAIT...!›
PTAAAAAANG
‹YOU DON'T GET TO HAVE THEM, ORC!!›
‹NOT THEM!!›
‹LISTEN TO ME, DAMMIT...!!›
NGH!!
FWAP
WHUMP

‹WILL YOU LISTEN *NOW*, DRAENEI?!›

‹KILL ME IF YOU PLEASE...BUT MY *WIFE*!›

‹MY *DAUGHTER*...!›

‹...HAVE NOTHING TO FEAR FROM ME.›

‹I...I DON'T UNDERSTAND...›

‹I DON'T EXPECT YOU TO. GO TO THEM.›

‹YOU'LL NEED THIS.›

‹THANK Y--›

SHHHTHUNK

YOU... YOU HAVE NO RIGHT...
TO CLAIM YOUR KILL?
YOU AND I ARE FROM THE SHADOWMOON CLAN, JARUK. WE TAKE WHAT WE WISH...AS GUL'DAN WILLS.
YOU WOULD DO WELL TO REMEMBER THAT. STILL...
HIH...HIH... HIH...

THE WORTHLESS BLUESKIN STILL DRAWS BREATH...I RELINQUISH THE HONOR.
FINISH HIM.
CAPTAIN!
IT APPEARS ONE OF THEM HAS ESCAPED! A FEMALE, BY THESE TRACKS.
AND HERE I THOUGHT THE EVENING'S ENTERTAINMENT WAS OVER...
FETCH THE MOUNTS!

RA'NOK, SEE TO THE DISPOSAL OF THE BODIES AND HAVE THE MEN SET UP CAMP ON THE RIDGE.
JARUK, FINISH THAT DRAENEI VERMIN AND THEN RIDE TO MEET ME.

I'LL TRY NOT TO **CARVE UP** THE **WENCH** TOO BADLY BEFORE YOU GET THERE.

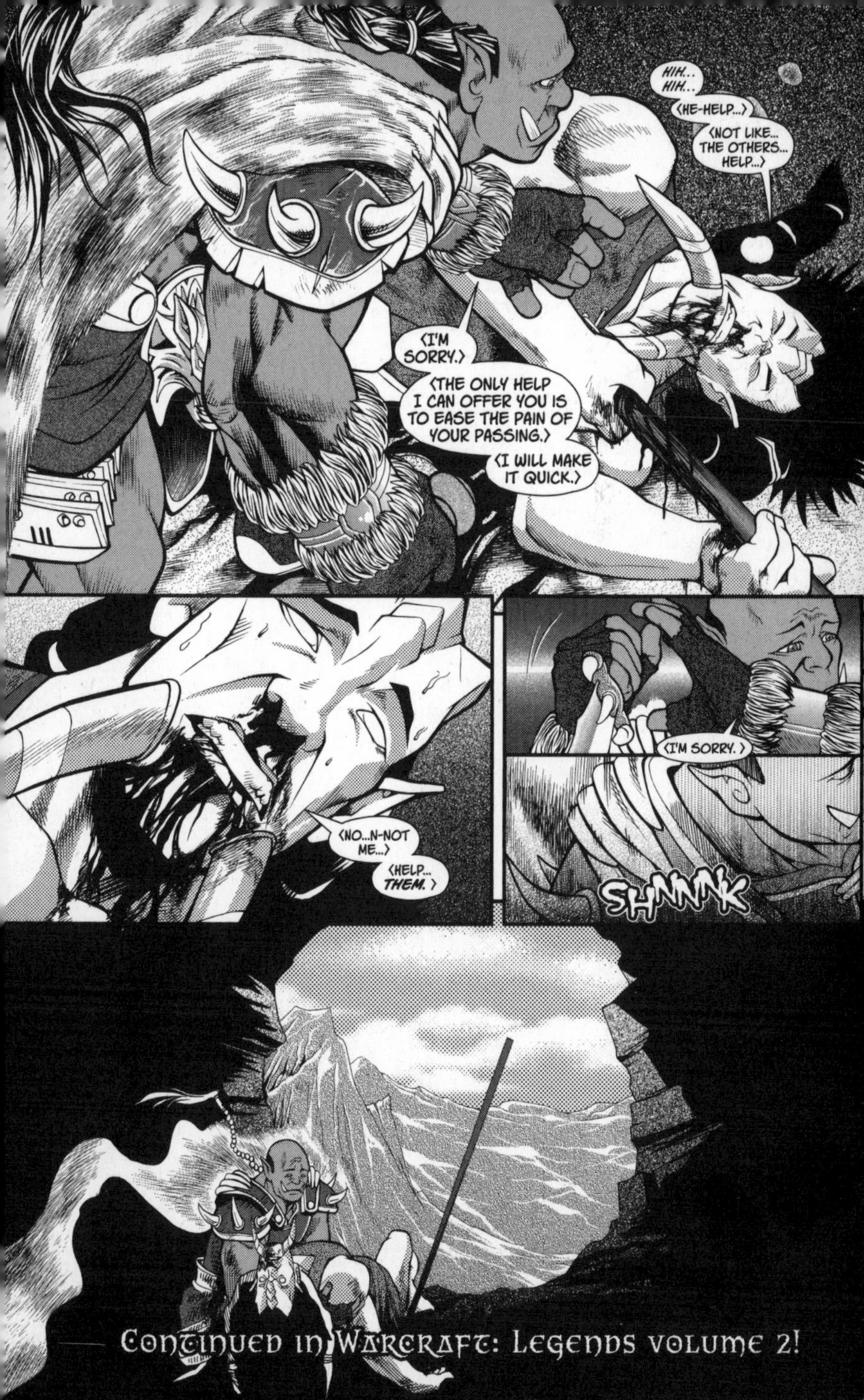

Continued in Warcraft: Legends volume 2!

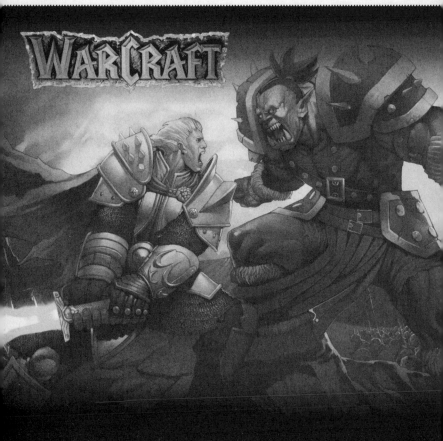

STARCRAFT®

AVAILABLE IN BOOKSTORES AUGUST 2008...AND BEYOND!

StarCraft: Frontline *Volume 1*

Check out www.TOKYOPOP.com/STARCRAFT
for exclusive news, updates and free downloadable art.

Art by: UDON with Saejin Oh

BUY IT WHEREVER BOOKS ARE SOLD

Actual Gameplay.
TEEN
T
Blood
Suggestive Themes
Use of Alcohol
Violence
ESRB CONTENT RATING www.esrb.org
Game Experience May Change
During Online Play